BEGINNER'S GUIDE TO DARKROOM TECHNIQUES

BEGINNER'S GUIDE TO
DARKROOM TECHNIQUES

Ralph Hattersley

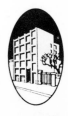

ROBERT HALE · LONDON

Copyright © 1976 by Ralph Hattersley
First published in Great Britain 1978
Reprinted 1979

ISBN 0 7091 6535 8

Robert Hale Limited
Clerkenwell House
Clerkenwell Green
London, EC1R 0HT

Printed in Great Britain by
Lowe & Brydone Printers Limited, Thetford, Norfolk

CONTENTS

CONTENTS

CONTENTS

BEGINNER'S GUIDE TO DARKROOM TECHNIQUES

TO JON, KATHI, AND BOB

HOW TO PREPARE AND EQUIP A DARKROOM

For developing film or making prints, you need a completely darkened place in which to work, because photographic films and papers are very sensitive to light. If any light whatever falls on film it will fog (turn dark), utterly ruining any pictures that are on it. Thus it must be taken from its cassette in total darkness. If ordinary light falls on printing paper it will also fog. However, there are special colored lights (safelights) that don't affect it. Though they are dim as well as colored, they provide good visibility and solve the fog problem.

The basic requirement for a developing and printing room is that there be some way of shutting out all light from outside, which may take time and ingenuity. It is far easier to wait until dark, when there is no light around. Then almost any kind of space will make an adequate darkroom. The kitchen is often the best place, because it has running water and work surfaces for enlarger, trays, printing paper, etc. Bathrooms are popular too, but they usually lack work surfaces. However, this can be remedied by moving in a card table and putting a piece of heavy plywood on top of the bathtub.

Running water is by no means a requirement for your workroom, because you can easily carry water anywhere in the house in a plastic bucket. Those who share your home with you may not like your tying up the kitchen or bathroom all evening or having to sit around with most of the lights out, so you should consider setting up in a more remote place and transporting your chemicals in a bucket. A corner of an attic or bedroom is fine. In warm weather you can even work in the garage or on an open back porch, provided there are no street lights nearby.

You may find waiting for nightfall inconvenient —especially in summer, when the days are long. If so, you should consider making a temporary or permanent daytime darkroom, which is actually fairly easy to do. You can effectively block out the light by covering windows and doors with heavy black paper held up with staples, pushpins, carpet tacks, or black masking tape.

A cheap, readily available, and effective type of black paper is roofing paper (tar paper), which you can buy at hardware or building-supply stores. It comes in long rolls that are thirty-six inches wide, which is wider than most door or window frames. There is enough in one inexpensive roll to last a lifetime. You can even block out the doors in a double garage and have most of a roll left over.

Though roofing paper is very heavy, you can easily cut it with ordinary sewing scissors. For a temporary darkroom, cut panels that fit to the edges of the door and window frames, then hold them up with pushpins. If too much light leaks around the edges, tape them down with masking tape. When you are through printing, remove the pushpins and tape, roll up the panels, and store them away for the next time. For a permanent darkroom, use staples or tacks and black tape.

Though roofing paper is most convenient, you can use any material that will block out light, including cardboard, wallboard, plywood, heavy black felt, black Con-Tact paper, craft paper, lead-lined window-shade material, black paint (for window panes), and heavy black plastic sheeting. However, some of these materials require the use of complicated tools, whereas you need only scissors for the black paper.

For a permanent darkroom, you should systematically trace down all light leaks through or around your panels, carefully plugging each one with black paper or tape. You will soon have a room in which you can safely remove film from its cassette. For a temporary darkroom, blocking every leak might prove inexpedient, because it could take you an hour or more each time.

For printing, it is nice to have a room that is absolutely dark until the safelights are turned on, yet this total darkness isn't really required. A *little* light leaking in won't do any harm. The question is, how much is a little? This rough check will easily tell you: Turn out all the lights in the room and wait about ten minutes, until your eyes are fully dark-adapted. If you can then *barely* make out the outlines of the things in the room, it is probably dark enough for printing. However, you shouldn't take printing paper out of its package and leave it lying around for more than a few seconds.

A darkroom made by light-trapping a window with black paper

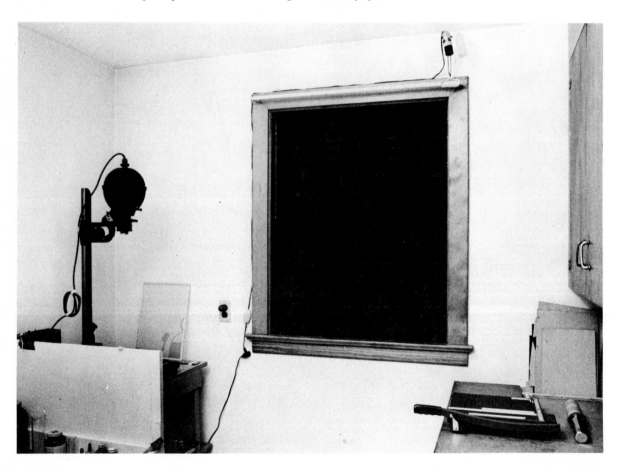

A room with this much light leaking in may or may not be dark enough for developing film, so you have to be careful, and there is a risk involved. You see, film is *much* more sensitive to light than photographic paper. Fortunately, there is a way in which we can use such a darkroom safely: by using a film-changing bag.

Since film has to be exposed to the air for only a short time when we are developing it, we need absolute darkness for just a few minutes. The critical period is when we are removing it from its cassette and putting it in a developing reel. Once it is in the developing tank it is safe, for tanks are absolutely lighttight.

With a film-changing bag, you can get through the critical steps very safely, even in a well-lighted room. It is a black, lighttight zippered bag with two elastic armholes. You put the film, reel, tank, and a beer-can opener (for opening the cassette) in it, then zipper it closed. Next, you put your hands and arms through the lighttight armholes, remove the film from its cassette, load it into the reel, put the reel in the tank, and put the cover on. Since the rest of the developing procedure can be carried out in daylight, you can see how the changing bag solves the problem of a darkroom that is not quite dark enough. However, don't buy one until you've tried to solve the problem of blacking out your workroom; you may not need it.

Most people have little choice in the room they can use for photography; they have to take whatever is available. Besides kitchens and bathrooms, people often use bedrooms, utility rooms, porches, garages, basement storage rooms, hallways, attics, and even walk-in closets. As we've seen, almost any area in a house or apartment will work, so long as the white light can be shut out.

The problem of finding work surfaces for the enlarger, trays, paper, etc., is a comparatively minor one, because almost any stable surface will do. You can use card tables, chairs, bureau tops, boards across sawhorses, wooden crates, shelves, stove and refrigerator tops, and so on. Even an ironing board will work well (for trays), provided it is shoved against the wall for stability.

Unfortunately, photographic chemicals may soften or curdle varnish and paint and can permanently stain Formica. You should therefore cover surfaces for your chemical trays with sheets of plastic, rubber, or roofing paper. Discarded plastic tablecloths, shower curtains, and tarpaulins are good and can easily be cut to any size. Saran Wrap and wax paper are fine. In a pinch you can use newspapers, but the chemicals soak through if you splash too much.

The chemicals are most destructive if they are left to stand for several days in puddles, for they will turn paint, varnish, and linoleum into a thick gravy. However, if you wipe them up right away they do no discernible damage, for they are slow-acting.

Most photographers like a darkroom to have a wet and a dry side. That is, chemicals and water are confined to one side, and things that must be

Using a film-changing bag to load film on a developing reel. In this lightproof zippered bag are a cassette of film, a beer-can opener, a developing reel, the developing tank, and the tank top. Absolute darkness prevails inside.

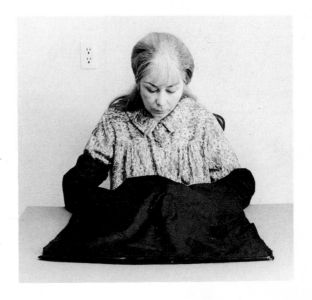

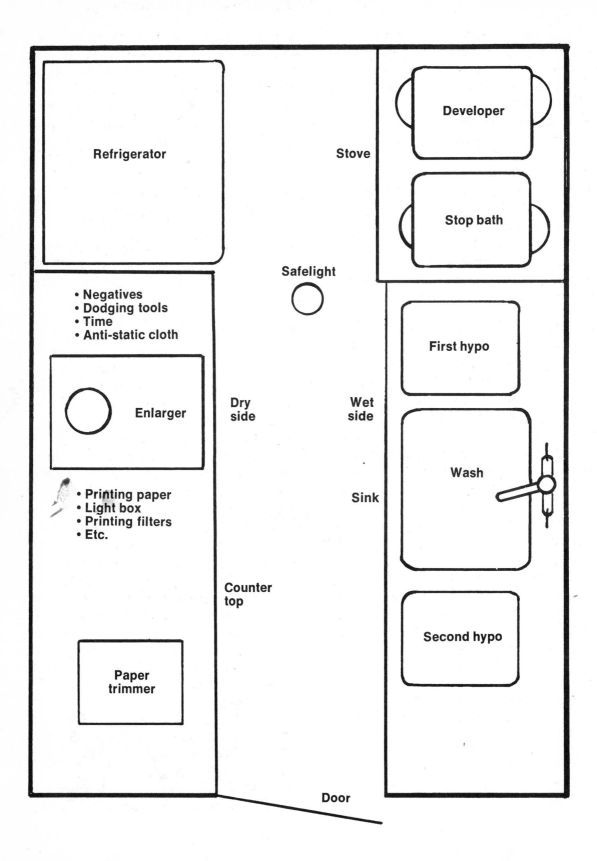

kept dry (enlarger, negatives, paper, etc.) to the other. We thus separate wet and dry things, because water and chemicals will ruin equipment and materials—even the enlarger, which only *looks* indestructible.

Unfortunately, many people haven't enough room for both a dry side and a wet side and may even have to line up their chemical trays right next to their enlargers. This is all right if you take great care to avoid any splashing whatever, though it is also a good idea to rig up high splashboards, or partitions, with cardboard and masking tape—just in case. The big problem here is that under the dim illumination of a safelight, people invariably splash a lot more than they think. Because they can't see the splashes, they assume they are not there, and by the time they discover them the damage may be done.

If possible, it is good to have two safelights, one near the enlarger and the other positioned directly over the print-developing tray. If you buy them from a photography store, ask for ones with either OC or S55-X filters, or shields, because they can be used with variable-contrast paper as well as the regular kind. However, you can save a lot of money by buying 7½-watt red GE bulbs and using them with ordinary cords or lamps. They also can be used with any paper, but they don't light up the developer tray quite as brightly. This is a bit frustrating, yet it won't affect the quality of your prints.

Though most inexpensive enlargers on the market today are quite good, the cheapest plastic models are a little flimsy. Therefore, it is best to invest as much as you can. Your best bet may be to buy a secondhand version of an expensive machine. If the lens is unscratched and the mechanical parts are in good working order, you can usually trust it, because there is not much that tends to go wrong in a good enlarger. A little rust on

the enlarger head or scratches on the baseboard will do no harm. Defective wiring, which is most often the only thing wrong, can easily be replaced. Indeed, a disreputable-looking machine may function splendidly—and sell for a song—provided it was a good enlarger to begin with. In contrast, when a very cheap enlarger decides to fall apart, it goes all the way and there is nothing you can do about it.

For print processing, you will need five plastic trays. If you intend to make 8×10 prints you can get along fine with 8×10 trays, though they do cramp you a little bit. If you have enough money and a large enough work space, buy the 11×14 size. I will explain later what the various trays are for.

When making prints, the paper is held in place with a special hinged frame called a printing easel. It will give white print borders of any width desired. Though easels are convenient, the good ones are also expensive, so don't buy one until you have read how you can easily make one for yourself (Appendix).

In making a print, you need a way of controlling the duration of its exposure to the enlarger light, for which special electric timers are usually used. Since they are quite expensive, consider buying a cheap, hand-wound metronome from a music store. It works just as well. A clock with a sweep second hand is very good. So is a watch with a sweep second hand, but you have to rig up a little darkroom spotlight in order to see the dial. It should show light only where you want it to. You can make one by taping a four-inch cylinder of black paper around the bulb end of a penlight. If you have to, you can time exposures by counting seconds under your breath, which is quite all right for many prints. However, some need more accurate timing.

For film processing, you will need a film reel and tank; a thermometer; a watch, clock, or timer, and a few other things, all of which will be discussed in the next chapter.

Most chemicals come in dry form. After they are mixed they should be stored in airtight bot-

Diagram showing how a kitchen can be used as a temporary darkroom

tles. Wine, juice, and cider bottles work very well. Plastic bottles, especially bleach containers, are not so good—unless you buy the special brown plastic bottles sold in photo stores. All in all, it is best to mix your chemicals in half-gallon quantities, unless you do a lot of work. Then you might find it more convenient to mix in gallon lots. You can also save quite a bit of money that way.

It is unnecessary at this point to explain the other things you will need for equipping your darkroom, but you will find it useful to have a partial list of them. At the appropriate time you will learn what everything is and how it should be used. Since the list is long you may find it frightening. However, most of the items aren't expensive. Though it will surely take you some time to gather everything together, you will never have to go through this particular hassle again.

A setup for making enlargements. A splashboard (on the left) protects the equipment from the chemicals.

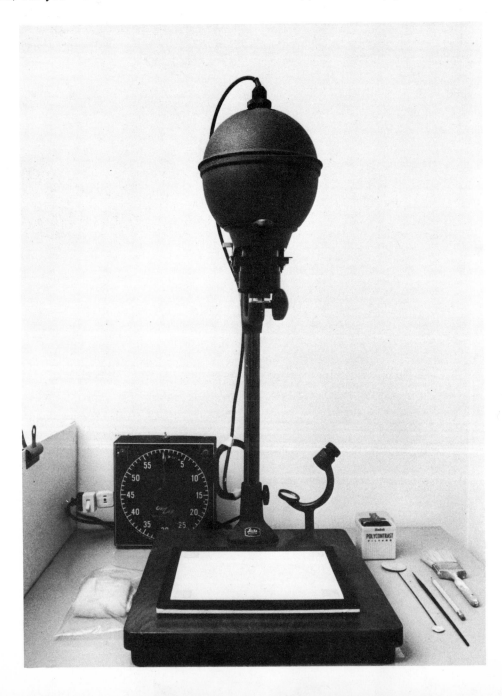

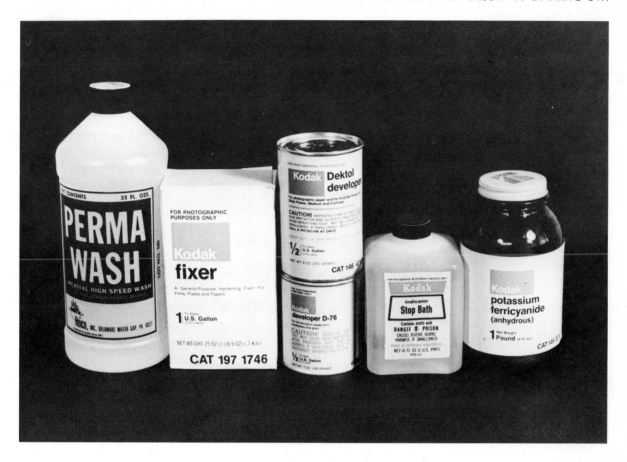

Some chemicals that are commonly used in photography

● **Photographic Equipment**

Enlarger
Enlarging easel (optional)
Photographic timer or metronome (optional)
Photographic sponge
Print-trimming board (optional)
Five print-processing trays, 8×10 or 11×14
Focus magnifier (optional)
Tray siphon (for washing prints) (optional)
Two print tongs, rubber-tipped bamboo (optional)
Photographic thermometer, preferably stainless steel

● **Photographic Chemicals**

D-76 film developer
Dektol print developer
Kodak Indicator Stop Bath
Regular acid-hardening fixing bath (hypo), in the dry form
Perma Wash (hypo eliminator), 1 quart
Potassium ferricyanide crystals (for bleaching), 1 pound
Kodak Photo-Flo solution, 1 pint
Kodak or Edwal hypo test kit (optional)
A spray can of Marshall's Film Klens (anti-static film cleaner)

● Miscellaneous Equipment

Two-gallon plastic pail (for mixing chemicals and carrying water)

Beer-can opener (for opening Kodak film cassettes)

Old turkish towels (for keeping fingers clean and dry)

Chemical stirring rod, stick, or large plastic spoon

Plastic or glass funnel, preferably with a filter

Glass or plastic measuring cup, pint or quart size

Several ordinary viscose sponges (for cleaning up)

Dodging and burning-in tools (homemade)

Lens-cleaning tissues (for cleaning enlarger lens and condenser)

Silicone negative- or record-cleaning cloth

Package of Q-Tips (for bleaching)

Package of surgical cotton (for bleaching)

Photographic spotting brush (for print retouching)

A no. 4 pointed sable brush (for cleaning negatives)

Bottle of black Spotone spotting dye

A plastic lemonade pitcher, gallon size

Four sheets of 12×16-inch single-strength glass (from the hardware store) (for making contact sheets)

Roll of 1-inch masking tape

Scissors

An 11×14-inch piece of ¾-inch plywood (for a borderless easel)

Roll of carpet tape (for easel)

White Con-Tact paper, 11×14 inches (for easel)

Two dozen rubber hose washers (for easel)

Small can of lighter fluid (for cleaning negatives)

Pint of rubbing alcohol (for cleaning negatives)

Bottles (for storing chemicals)

Comet or Ajax-type cleanser (for cleaning trays)

Paper towels (for bleaching and print retouching)

One ounce of Kodak black opaque (for negative retouching)

Depending on what you wish to do with your photography, there may be other things you will need. However, our list has already reached a terrifying length, so I will mention additional items only at the appropriate places in the book. After learning what they are for, you can decide for yourself whether to invest in them.

Be sure you understand that the things listed as optional actually *are* optional. That is, you can get along very well without them or use homemade, but very effective, substitutes, thus saving yourself a substantial amount of money. If you are ingenious you can even make your own enlarger, though it is not listed here as optional.

HOW TO DEVELOP FILM

A roll of film is a long strip of thin plastic that is coated on one side with toughened gelatin containing light-sensitive silver compounds in the form of extremely small crystals. We call them light-sensitive because they can be chemically changed by light.

When you take a picture, the light reflected by various parts of your subject passes through the camera lens, which focuses it on the film. There the light forms a visible image of your subject in complete detail. If you could stand inside your camera you would see that it looks like a projected color slide. It is important to understand that this image on the film is composed entirely of light and nothing else, and that some parts of it are brighter than others. For example, a white cat will show up brighter than a black dog.

Try to understand that the image lying on the surface of the film is *light energy,* with the white cat having a lot of it and the black dog very little or none. In the area of gelatin beneath the cat the silver compounds will be acted on by a lot of this light energy and thus be chemically changed to a considerable degree. In the area beneath the black dog there will be little or no change.

Though these chemical changes are real they aren't visible at this point. The cat, the dog, and their environment have formed a "latent image" in the gelatin, not a visible one. This means, how-

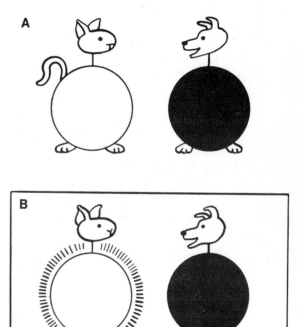

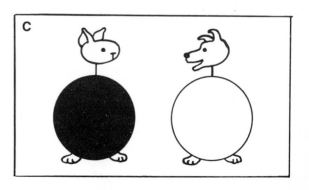

ever, that it is a *potentially* visible one, provided that it is treated with a chemical developer.

If a section of the film has been acted on by a sufficient amount of light energy it can be chemically developed. That is, a developer will break up the light-energized silver compounds, converting them into certain gases, which escape, and pure metallic silver, which happens to be black. The image, now fully visible, is made entirely of this black silver. Of course, the more silver an area contains the darker it is, and vice versa. Areas with none at all are transparent.

Crystals insufficiently exposed to light will not be developed. Since they are still light-sensitive they must be gotten rid of somehow. Otherwise, on exposure to light they will soon turn black, completely obliterating the image. It is the function of the fixing bath to take care of this problem, which it does by changing the light-sensitive silver crystals into a hypo-silver compound. This new compound is entirely insensitive to light. Furthermore, it is water-soluble, so we can rid the gelatin of it completely by washing the film in running water.

When you examine developed film you will see that the tones of your subject are reversed. For example, our white cat is now black, the black dog white (clear or transparent). For this reason we call a developed film image a "negative." Though the logic behind this is unclear, it is standard photographic jargon nonetheless. The gelatin part of film (or paper) is the "emulsion." The fixing bath is usually called "hypo."

Momentarily letting a light-image fall on the film in your camera is "exposure" or "making an exposure." When we are printing we "make exposures" by turning on the enlarger light. The light-sensitive compounds that we use are "silver halides," such as silver bromide and silver iodide.

The jargon is an important part of photography, but I am introducing it as gradually as possible. Learn the terms as fast as you can, because they will help you to read photography books and magazines, and to communicate with others interested in photography.

• Things You Need to Develop Film

Exposed film
Developing tank and reel
Photographic thermometer
Timer, clock, or watch
Funnel (glass or plastic)
Measuring cup (glass or plastic)
Photographic sponge
String
Clothespins
Towel
Scissors
Beer-can opener
Glassine negative sleeves
D-76 developer solution
Fixing solution (hypo)
Perma Wash solution (optional)
Photo-Flo solution (optional)
Water
Stirring rod, stick, or plastic spoon
Plastic bucket
Storage bottles for D-76 and hypo solutions

Developing tanks and reels: The ones most recommended for both beginners and advanced photographers are the GAF (Anscomatic), Paterson, and Nikor types. The easiest to use is the GAF, closely followed by the Paterson. The most difficult (the problem is in loading the film in the reels) is the Nikor, but it is the most popular among advanced amateurs and professionals.

You can develop only one roll of film at a time in a GAF tank, but the Paterson and Nikor tanks come in various sizes, holding up to seven reels (Paterson) and sixteen (Nikor). Developing so much film at once is quite awkward, however, so if you wish to process more than one roll at a time you should settle for either the Paterson five-reel or the Nikor four-reel. I am referring here to 35-mm reels.

The GAF and Paterson tanks and reels are plastic, the Nikor stainless steel. However, the different reels are equally fragile, so that drop-

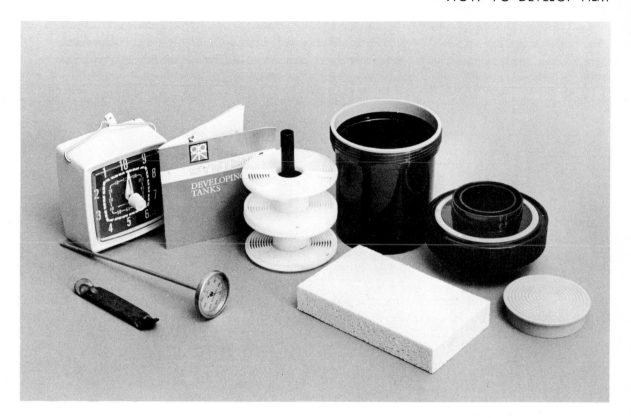

Equipment for developing film: (front) beer-can opener, photographic thermometer, photographic sponge; (rear) photographic timer, Paterson instruction manual, two Paterson "walk-in" reels, developing tank, tank top, and tank cap

ping one of them on the floor may ruin it. Nevertheless, with proper care the Nikor equipment will last for fifty years or more. Plastic tanks will last for years too, but they show signs of wear sooner, and plastics eventually deteriorate, even when not in use. You may in time have a warping problem with a GAF reel, which is made of ordinary plastic, but the Paterson nylon reel won't tend to warp.

The adjustable GAF and Paterson reels will accept various film sizes, including 120, 620, 127, 35-mm, 828, and 126 (cartridge-load). With Nikor we have non-adjustable reels in two sizes, one for 120 and 620, the other for 35-mm, 828,

and 126. As you see, Nikor reels cannot handle the 127 size, but few people use it now, anyway.

Thermometer: If you can afford it, buy a stainless-steel one. Glass thermometers break easily, and the thick ones take much too long to register changes in temperature.

Photographic sponge: Used for wiping water off processed film before hanging it up to dry. Since it has unusually fine texture it does this well, whereas ordinary viscose sponges do not.

Glassine negative envelopes: Used for storing and protecting negatives. Though you can use ordinary business envelopes or make your own negative sleeves out of typing paper, it isn't wise. In almost all papers, sulfur compounds are used as preservatives. In time they will degrade or destroy film images. So if you want your negatives to last your lifetime, buy the special envelopes, or sleeves.

Developer: Though there are numerous good developers available, the only one recommended here is Kodak D-76, a classical formula of great popularity. It is good, dependable, moderately fine-grain, and has a good "shelf life," which means that it can be stored in solution for several months without significant deterioration. In contrast, some developers "fall apart" rather rapidly. Though classified by Kodak as having "moderately fine grain," D-76 is used in certain custom labs for 35-mm film that is to be enlarged to mural size, which indicates that moderately fine is quite fine enough.

Fixing solution (hypo): Use either a regular acid-hardening fixing solution or a "rapid" (or "quick") fixer. Any brand will do, and you can buy it in either the dry chemical or solution form, though the dry form is cheaper. To save even more money, buy the one-gallon size.

Perma Wash: The best available "hypo eliminator," made by the Heico company. It will save you a good deal of time in washing both negatives and prints and help insure their longevity. By radically cutting down on the "wet time" it inhibits the development of graininess in negatives.

Photo-Flo: Like a dishwashing detergent, Photo-Flo breaks down the surface tension of water so that it will slide right off film rather than cling in large drops. Through tiny drops are all right, large ones cause ugly "drying marks" that are impossible to remove. If you soak your film in Photo-Flo just before hanging it up to dry, you don't have to use a sponge. However, you can use both if you wish.

● Getting the Developer Ready

Any kind of *film* developer that is sold in powder form should be mixed at least a day before you intend to use it, though the ones sold in liquid form can be used right away. All *paper* developers, however, can be used for printing as soon as they are mixed. D-76 comes as a powder, so mix it ahead of time. Using it too soon will lead to substantial overdevelopment, too much contrast, and a considerable amount of "grain" (a granular, or sandy, condition caused by the clumping together of silver particles).

The mixed developer is called the "stock" solution; for the "working" solution you dilute it with water 1:1 (half and half). If the D-76 is too cold (see chart), dilute it with warm water; too warm, dilute it with cold. If you wish to adjust the developer temperature *after* it has been diluted, use a one-gallon plastic food-storage bag filled with either ice cubes or hot water, stirring it around in the developer until the temperature is right. This way, you don't dilute the developer further.

Time and Temperature Film Developing Chart for D-76 Diluted 1:1

	Tri-X	Plus-X	Verichrome Pan
65F	11½ min	8½ min	9 min
68F	10	7¼	8½
70F	9	6½	7
72F	8¼	6	6¼
75F	7¼	5¼	5½

Some people prefer to make their developer dilutions right in the developing tank, others to do it in a pitcher or graduate. Since a film tank has a lighttight pour-in top, you can put the loaded film reel in a dry tank, shut out the light by putting on the top, then pour in the developer whenever you get around to it. Beginners generally prefer to do it this way, so that they won't panic in the dark. Advanced photographers do it the other way, putting the reel in the filled tank and capping it while still in the dark. This way, there is a little less chance of getting air bubbles on the film, which can cause little round spots on negatives.

● Time and Temperature

In photography, time and temperature controls are often critical, so you should never forget them. In film processing, you should combine exactly the right developing time with exactly the right developer temperature, or things will go awry. You can use different times and temperatures, but they must work together. For example, with a warm developer you use a short time, with a colder one a longer time—but you don't do this in an arbitrary way. Instead, you should carefully follow the time and temperature figures on our chart.

Do not suppose that you can accurately gauge temperature with your finger, because your judgment can easily be ten to fifteen degrees off without your noticing a thing. *Use a thermometer! Never guess,* or you will surely rue the day.

The time and temperature figures on our chart apply only to development in tanks of the types recommended in this book. For larger ones you need revised data.

The films charted are the only ones recommended. Kodak Tri-X and Plus-X are long-time favorites of the professionals, and most inexpensive cameras are specifically designed for use with either Plus-X or Verichrome Pan. So stick with these names and save yourself trouble. Whatever you do, don't buy off-brand, discount film, for it is usually years out of date and the photographic equivalent of a rotten egg.

In developing film be sure to stick within the recommended 65- to 75-degree temperature range, using the plastic-bag trick to bring your developer to temperature, if necessary. Below 65 degrees, developers lose much of their activity. Above 75, one of the ingredients (hydroquinone) may get too active, causing fog. And the emulsion gets too soft, so that it is easily damaged.

It is advisable to bring all solutions (rinse, hypo, wash water) to the same temperature as the developer, though a variation of two to three degrees in either direction is all right. You will get finer grain by thus limiting the temperature range. Once you've gotten all solutions to temperature, you can hold them there by setting their containers in a water bath, which is simply a deep tray of water at the desired temperature. Without this over-all temperature control you might have a coarse-grain problem, depending mainly on the type of film you are using and *how much* the temperatures vary from solution to solution. However, proper control takes the guesswork out of it.

● Film Handling

You have seen that film is a plastic strip with an emulsion on one side. Until the film has been processed the emulsion is sensitive to both light and your body chemistry (and numerous other things). Thus, if you touch the emulsion side you are likely to get permanent fingerprints—so don't touch it! It is all right to touch the other side (the "backing side") with clean dry hands, however.

Since both sides feel the same to your touch it is necessary to remember how film is loaded on its spool, which is always emulsion side in. Thus if you remove film from a cassette and pick up the spool, you know you are touching only the backing side, which is safe.

It would be wise to buy a practice roll at a photo store. It is out-of-date film sold at a large discount for people who wish to examine film in the daylight to see how it is spooled, then use it to practice loading their developing reels. Playing with just one roll can save you a lot of agony in the dark.

● Loading Your Developing Reel

Since the GAF, Paterson, and Nikor tank and reel sets come with excellent instructions it would be senseless to repeat them here. However, customers sometimes steal the instruction sheets, so make sure one is included with your purchase. And when you get it home take care not to lose it, lest after a lapse of a month or two you forget how to load and have to learn anew.

Paterson and GAF reels are of the "walk-in" type. You push one end of your film under a spring-loaded pin in the feed gate of the reel. Then you start twisting one flange of the reel back and forth, and this "walks" the film right into it, as easy as pie. Be sure to note the line in your instructions that tells you to round off the corners of the film with scissors. Otherwise, it is liable to jam.

Since the Nikor reel is considerably harder to load, you had better study the instructions carefully and be sure to work with a practice roll. First, load it several times while watching yourself in the daylight, next do it with your eyes closed, and, finally, do it several times in the dark. Without this practice you are very likely to come a cropper. If you start right out with exposed film it may jump its channels, so that some of your pictures will get stuck together in the developer. However, Nikor equipment is excellent, so don't let this dire warning make you shy away from it. But do your homework with your practice roll!

● Agitation

When you develop film it is necessary to "agitate" (stir up the developer) for five seconds every thirty seconds, which you do by simply moving the tank around. However, for the *first* thirty seconds of development the agitation should be continuous, mainly to get rid of air bubbles. If you let the tank just sit there you will get bubble marks ("air bells"), and the casual eddy currents in the developer will cause a disagreeable mottle on your negatives.

How you agitate can make a difference, too. The consensus among photographers is that the best method is to completely invert the developing tank, but this technique can cause development marks of another type. What we need is to randomize agitation, because random movement of the developer within the tank will give you very even development. The best bet is to use three different agitation methods. Use one for each 5-second agitation period, then repeat the sequence until the developing time is up. For the initial 30-second period, just perform the entire sequence twice.

This schedule of thirty seconds' agitation to start, followed by five seconds' agitation every thirty seconds, is a carefully worked out optimal technique. Don't agitate more than that or you'll get development marks of still another kind.

Method one: Invert the tank three or four times during the 5-second period. Method two: Rapidly spin the tank like a top, first clockwise, then counterclockwise, for the next period. Method three: Rapidly slide the tank back and forth on the table, for a distance of about one foot. When they are thus used in rotation, these three methods will give you very even development.

The GAF tank is designed so that it doesn't need to be inverted, spun, or slid back and forth. To agitate, you rapidly twist the little thermometer stirring rod that is provided. This will give you evenly developed negatives.

Film should also be agitated for its first thirty seconds in the fixing bath (hypo). Unless you do this you may have a problem with other types of processing defects. After the thirty seconds, however, you can let the tank just sit there until the fixing time is up.

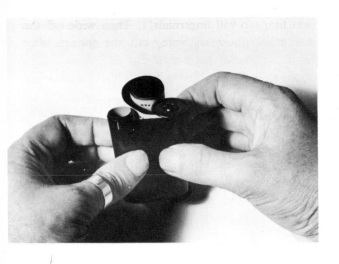

Separating roll film from its paper backing, taking care not to touch the emulsion side

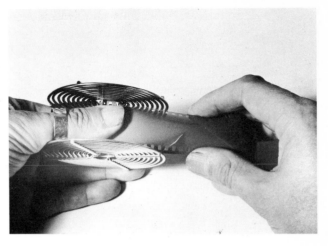

The initial step in loading a Nikor reel

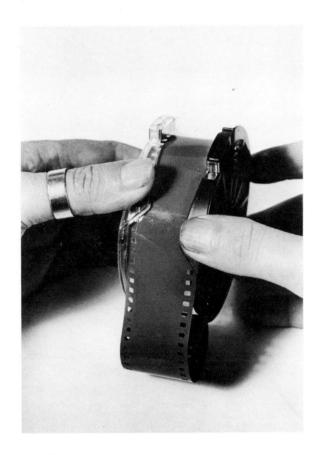

Loading film in a GAF reel. Twisting one flange of the reel "walks" the film right into it.

• Step by Step Film Processing

1. In total darkness, load the film reel and put it in the tank. Put the cover on and check to see that it is on all the way.

2. Turn on the room light.

3. Dilute the D-76 developer 1:1 and check the temperature, adjusting it if necessary.

4. Refer to the developing chart for the proper developing time and set the timer (if you are using one).

5. Put a container of water and another of hypo in a convenient place near the developing tank.

6. Pour the developer in the tank and start the timer (or check your watch).

7. Carefully following the agitation schedule and methods given, develop the film until only forty-five seconds remain of the preselected developing time.

8. Immediately pour the developer down the drain, discarding it, and fill the tank with water at the correct temperature. As soon as it is full, pour the water out again.

9. Immediately fill the tank with hypo and agitate vigorously for the first thirty seconds. After ten more minutes, pour the hypo *back into its storage bottle*. If you are using rapid fix, cut the time to five minutes. You may now take the top off the tank, because the film is no longer sensitive to light.

10. While it is still on the reel and in the tank, wash the film in rapidly running water at the right temperature for thirty seconds (or pour in five changes of water from a bucket).

11. Pour in a temperature-adjusted Perma Wash bath (¾ ounce per quart of water) and agitate ten seconds. After a total of thirty seconds, pour out the Perma Wash.

12. Wash the film for another thirty seconds in running water (or change the water five times).

13. Pour in a Photo-Flo solution, also temperature-adjusted, for one minute.

14. Hang up the film to dry.

You remove film from a Kodak 35-mm cassette by prying the end off the cassette with a beer-can opener. For a 126 plastic cartridge, twist it until it cracks open. For larger film sizes, unroll them and separate them from their paper backings. If you have done your homework with your practice roll you already know these things.

The reason for pouring out the developer when there is still forty-five seconds left of the developing time is that residual developer in the emulsion will continue to act all the way through the water rinse. Thus by the time you pour in the hypo the film will have completely developed.

If you are not using Perma Wash your film should wash for at least twenty minutes, though that is cutting the time rather short.

If you wish, you can wipe off your film with a photographic sponge and not use Photo-Flo. If so, thoroughly soak the sponge several minutes ahead of time, then squeeze it out as dry as you can get it just before use. With your hand, vigorously brush off the wiping surface to make sure there is no grit on it, because it will easily scratch wet film (so will fingernails!). Then wipe off the film three times, squeezing out the sponge after each time. Hang the film up to dry.

You make a film-drying line with string and clothespins. The best place for it is in a room where there is little dust and traffic, the bathroom usually being the best bet. If there is dust there, turn on the hot water in the tub or shower for a few minutes; a little steam will settle the dust. The problem with dust is that it easily gets embedded in wet gelatin and is hard to remove.

After hanging up a roll of film, weight its lower end with a clothespin. Check to see that there are no large water drops (tiny droplets are all right), for they make drying marks. If you find some, pick them off with your fingers or the sponge. Do this also with dust specks.

To remove film from a Nikor reel, just pull it out, letting the reel turn in your hand. With Paterson and GAF reels, pull the flanges apart a little way.

● Care of Negatives

When your film has dried, you should cut it into short strips of images (frames). Strips of five frames are convenient for 35-mm, six for 126, and three for 120. These short strips makes negatives easier to handle when you are printing them. It is also easier to make contact sheets with them (next chapter).

After cutting, you should immediately put your negatives in glassine sleeves, but only one per sleeve, because bunching them up will cause scratches.

Negatives are extremely susceptible to scratches, fingerprints, and abrasions, which show up as ugly marks on your prints. Therefore, you should always handle them by their edges, lay them down only on clean surfaces, and keep them in their sleeves when they are not being printed. Do not store film by rolling it up, because this usually causes scratches. Keep it in a cool, dry place, because heat and humidity will eventually ruin negatives.

HOW TO MAKE AND USE CONTACTS
EXPOSURE   HOW TO PROCESS PRINTS
NEGATIVE AND PAPER CONTRAST

There are two basic ways of making prints: by projection and by contact printing. The first involves projecting a negative image onto printing paper; the resulting print is called an enlargement, or projection print. For the second way you lay the negative right on top of the paper and make an exposure. The result is called a contact, contact print, or contact proof. The contact is used mainly for previewing pictures before enlarging them and is one of the photographer's most useful tools. One usually contacts a whole roll of negatives on a single piece of printing paper and can thus see at a glance how they all stack up. Note that the word "contact" comes from the fact that the negatives and paper are in actual contact during exposure.

● **Things You Need**

Four sheets of 12×16-inch single-strength glass
Soap, hot water, and a towel
Masking tape
Enlarger
Timer, metronome, or watch
Safelight(s)

Enlarging paper (not *contact* paper), double weight
Thermometer
Dektol print developer
Kodak Indicator Stop Bath
First hypo bath
Second hypo bath
Perma Wash
Tray siphon (optional)
Photographic blotters (optional)
Five processing trays
Paper towels
Scissors
China-marker pencil
Lighter fluid
Magnifying glass or illuminated magnifier

In these lists of "Things You Need" you will often find items repeated. This is so you won't have to skip back and forth in the book looking for things when you need them.

Glass: The four sheets are used together to make a single heavy, loosely laminated plate of glass. In making contact prints there must be very close contact between the negatives and the printing paper; for sharp pictures they must be tightly squeezed together. To get good contact you put the negatives emulsion (dull side) down on the emulsion of the paper (shiny side), then press them flat with a plate of glass. One thickness of glass is enough if you hold opposite sides of it down with your hands.

However, this may be inconvenient, because you have to start holding it down before you begin the exposure, and this doesn't leave you a free hand to turn on the enlarger light. The answer is a foot switch, which you probably don't have. Another answer is to have a plate of glass heavy enough to flatten the negatives (which often curl like steel springs) all by itself. Heavy plate glass will do very nicely, but it is very expensive and easily scratched. So we create its equivalent with four sheets of ordinary single-strength glass in the standard 12×16-inch size. It is both cheap and durable.

When you are buying your glass at the hardware store, check each piece to see that it has no bubbles or scratches, because they would show up in your prints. Today's glass is very well made, so you should have no problem. The easiest way to check is to hold the glass in front of a flatly lighted section of a wall or ceiling.

Later, wash each piece carefully with soap and water (don't use a glass cleaner), then wipe it completely dry with a turkish towel. Next, stack up the plates of glass, taking great care not to get dust or lint between them. Finally, tape them together along the edges with masking tape. Don't squeeze them into the tightest possible contact while you are taping, however, for that will cause colored, irregular rings. Just let them lie there while you are doing it. Only the negatives and the printing paper need tight contact, not the individual pieces of glass.

Enlarging papers: Enlarging papers are made for use with enlarger light sources, which usually aren't very intense. Thus the papers are made very light-sensitive in order to compensate. In comparison, *contact* papers are very "slow" (relatively insensitive to light), because they are

used to make contact prints of large negatives in special contact printers that have very intense light sources. Though you intend to make contact prints, you will be using the enlarger as a light source—so use enlarging paper.

Thermometer: In making contacts or enlargements your need for a thermometer is not nearly as great as it is in film processing. In fact, most people seldom use one in printing, unless the temperatures are obviously very high or very low. The safe temperature range is from about 65 to 90 degrees F, though it is better to stay in the 65–75-degree range if you can.

Dektol print developer: Print and film developers are not the same, so don't try interchanging them unless you know exactly what you are doing. For prints, a developer has to be very alkaline and active, while lower-alkalinity film developers are much less active. Thus, if you use a paper developer for film you can easily get heavy overdevelopment. In contrast, a print in film developer may take an hour or more to develop.

Kodak Dektol is a variant of Kodak D-72, a classical formula in photography. It is dependable, has good keeping qualities, holds up for a considerable time in the developing tray, and works well with all brands and types of contact and enlarging papers. With most papers it produces a very neutral print color, which most people find desirable.

• Setting Up the Trays

Chemical trays are usually arranged touching one another in a row, or "processing line." This is convenient and cuts down the amount of splashing and dripping, but it isn't absolutely necessary. If you lack space, put your trays wherever you can, even under the enlarger table or scattered around the room.

Line up your trays in this order (if you can): (1) developer, (2) stop bath, (3) first hypo, (4) second hypo, and (5) water. Dilute the Dektol stock solution 1:2 (one part Dektol, two of water). Use one-half ounce of stock indicator stop bath per quart of water, or two ounces per gallon. The hypo stock solution should not be diluted.

As we've seen, the temperatures in a print-processing line aren't very critical. Temperature variations from tray to tray also matter little, because print emulsions are much less susceptible to damage than film emulsions; and there is no grain problem with printing paper, which is nearly grainless.

To make print handling easier, fill all the trays to within one-half inch or so of their tops. Take great care not to dribble stop bath or hypo into the developer, for they can ruin it in a jiffy. Conversely, developer will ruin both stop bath and hypo. However, the stop bath is used as an intentional sacrifice designed to save the hypo from destruction.

Here's how it works. When a print is transferred from the developer to the stop bath it carries with it some of the developer solution, which is alkaline. However, the alkali is ruinous to hypo, which can function only if it is acidic. The stop bath, a dilute acid, acidifies the print so that it won't undermine the effectiveness of the hypo. Since the stop bath itself is eventually ruined by the developer it is important to know when it is no longer functioning properly. For this we have a chemical indicator. When this yellow bath begins to turn purple (the indicator), discard it and mix a fresh one.

Concentrated indicator stop bath is very strong, so you should add it to the water—not the other way around. Pouring water into a strong acid can result in its exploding into your eyes, a very unpleasant prospect.

As far as possible, arrange your trays so as to minimize dribbling or splashing onto the work surfaces and floor. From your waist, hang a towel for keeping your fingers dry and dripless. When you *do* splash, as you most probably will, use paper towels for the wipe-up. If you use your turkish towel for this it will soon get contaminated, so that you will be wiping your fingers dirty instead of clean, thus leading you to con-taminating everything you touch. Remember this: in photography, cleanliness is next to godliness.

• Getting to Know Your Enlarger

An enlarger is very much like a slide projector and can even be used for slides in a pinch. It has a light source (bulb), a light-condensing system, a focusing system, a system for raising or lowering it on its standard, and a lens with a variable aperture. Usually these systems are combined in such a simple way that it is quite obvious what they all do. If you have used an enlarger to make even one print it is unlikely you'll ever forget how it works.

The only hard thing to understand is how you are supposed to use the variable aperture. This is something you literally *have* to know, so we will go into it in some depth. The aperture is merely a variable-size hole, resembling somewhat the iris diaphragm of the eye. It is even called the diaphragm, or iris diaphragm. We can make this hole large, small, or set it to a limitless range of sizes in between. However, it is "graduated," so that if you wish you can easily set it to certain sizes that are related to one another in a very specific and accurate way. Though the relationship is extremely simple it is quite difficult to understand at first, so you will have to bear down a bit here.

These graduations—called "stops," "f/stops," or "f-numbers"—are marked on the outside of the lens barrel. Some lenses make a clicking sound as they are moved through each position and are thus said to have "click stops." It is a lot easier to hear clicks than to see the marks under a safelight. Don't let the jargon distress you, because it merely refers to a simple relationship of areas. By opening or closing the aperture we are merely changing the area of a hole.

Unfortunately, the numbers at the stop settings seem to be backward, because a large number stands for a small hole and vice versa. This is because these figures are actually ratios, which you needn't worry about right now. Though things aren't backward, they seem to be, and that is what you have to get used to.

On your enlarger lens barrel you have a scale of f-number (f/stop, or aperture) settings: f/4—f/5.6—f/8—f/11—f/16. Your lens may start with f/5.6, but don't let that worry you. Changing the setting from left to right on the scale is called "stopping down," because the hole gets progressively smaller. Moving in the other direction, or "opening up," makes it larger, of course. All you have to remember is this: The larger the number the smaller the hole.

We have just seen that moving from f/4 toward f/16 is called stopping down, because the aperture (hole) gets progressively smaller. Thus, making one jump, say from f/4 to f/5.6, is "stopping down one stop." If we should go in the other direction, say all the way from f/16 to f/4, that would be "opening up *four* stops." These unfamiliar terms and numbers are an important part of the photographer's jargon, so try to get them straight.

In using the aperture settings (hole sizes), we are most interested in how their areas relate, which is as follows: As we progressively go from f/4 to f/5.6 to f/8 to f/11 to f/16 we cut the area exactly in half with each jump. Conversely, if we go in the other direction we double the area each time. Though the f-numbers themselves are ratios (fractions) and not measures of areas, the relationships just given hold true, nonetheless. And this is all we need to know.

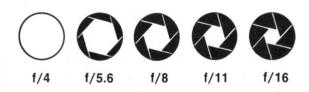

f/4   f/5.6   f/8   f/11   f/16

Diagrammatic representation of the f-number settings in your enlarger lens

• Exposure

In printing, our chief interest in the progressive doubling or halving of the area of the aperture is that it gives us some control over the "exposure." The concept of exposure is one of the most important notions in photography, so we had better look into it. It is important to remember that "exposure" (or *"an* exposure") always consists of *two* things: light intensity and time. This is usually written as: Exposure=Light Intensity×Time (or $E=I\times T$). This is the famous "Law of Reciprocity," and all of photography is based on it.

The $\times$ in this formula merely indicates that you can get the *same* exposure with many different combinations of light intensity and time. For example, it is possible to move from using a lot of light and little time to using a little light and a lot of time without changing the exposure at all. It is like saying that 10×2 is quantitatively the *same as* 2×10, which it obviously is.

In order to make use of the Law of Reciprocity (which we do every time we make a print or shoot a picture) we must have adequate control over both light intensity and time. The intensity of the enlarger bulb itself doesn't change. However, we can use the variable aperture to control the amount of light that actually passes through the lens. With a timer or metronome we can easily control the amount of time for which the enlarger light is turned on. Thus we can have as many combinations as we wish of light intensity and time.

• Correct Exposure

At this point it is necessary to distinguish between "exposure" and *"correct* exposure," which can be miles apart in certain respects. Exposure is any combination whatever of light intensity and time. Whenever you let light fall upon film or printing paper you get an exposure, even if you don't consider the light intensity or the amount of time, and even if the images come out much too light or too dark. In contrast, "correct exposure" is the combination of light intensity and time that will make an image come out just the way you want it to. This definition is simple and subjective, as you can see, but that's really all there is to it.

• Correct Exposure in Printing

We will now see how one manipulates the light intensity and time controls in printing. Let us say you have made a test strip (pages 55ff.) and determined that the "correct exposure" for your picture is two seconds at f/4. Now, a two-second exposure is not so good, because timers and metronomes can't be used with accuracy in such a short time span, and it doesn't permit us to dodge or burn-in (pages 71ff.). So you decide that you need a longer time without changing the exposure.

The method is simple. You find that you can use longer times by merely stopping down the lens to reduce the intensity of the light passing through it. Without changing the exposure at all, this would give you the following light-intensity-and-time combinations: f/4 (two seconds)—f/5.6 (four seconds)—f/8 (eight seconds)—f/11 (sixteen seconds)—f/16 (thirty-two seconds). Both eight and sixteen seconds are convenient exposure times, while four is still too short and thirty-two tediously long.

If a print were to come out too dark or too light you would want a *different* exposure, of course. We can correct for a dark print by stopping down, cutting the time, or both. We correct for a light one by opening up, increasing the time, or both.

This rather heavy material on exposure was made necessary by the fact that beginners generally get badly confused in this area—and you can now see why. Furthermore, it is of fundamental importance in learning to see how photography actually works. The chapter on test strips will help clarify things for you, as will a little experience in making pictures.

• More About Enlargers

Before we leave this section you need to know a little more about enlargers. For example, enlarger lenses aren't very "sharp" when used "wide open" (opened to the largest aperture). That is, they produce images that are fuzzy, or diffuse, near their edges. For better sharpness it is usually good to stop down either two or three stops. However, even going down one stop is a considerable improvement. Stopping down more than three isn't wise, because enlarger lenses aren't very sharp at their smallest apertures, either.

You shouldn't leave the enlarger light turned on longer than you can help. It shortens the life of the bulb. If the bulb gets hot enough it may burn out the insulation in its socket and possibly damage the condenser or lens. A hot enlarger may destroy a negative left in it.

Photographic chemicals are excellent conductors of electricity, so if you get them on your enlarger you may short it and shock yourself cross-eyed. They will also corrode it, as will water itself.

The alignment of the enlarger standard and the baseboard is critical if you want prints that are sharp from edge to edge. Since it is easily thrown off, you shouldn't handle your enlarger roughly or drop it on the floor. Though you might be able to get it back into alignment again it could take you all day.

You should frequently clean the lens and condenser with lens tissue. In fact, you might do it every time you set up for printing.

• Exposing the Contact Sheet

Raise the enlarger head to the top of its standard, then stop the lens down two or three stops. Turn off all lights except the safelight(s). Cut off a one-inch strip of printing paper and place it *emulsion up* on the enlarger baseboard. Put a single strip of negatives *emulsion down* on top of the paper and hold them in tight contact with the glass plate.

Expose a test strip as follows: Give the *whole strip* a five-second exposure. Then start progressively *covering it up* in one-inch jumps with the printing-paper package. At each position give it an additional five-second exposure. Then process the strip (next section) and pick the step with the best-looking image, neither too light nor too dark. Count up by fives from the bottom to the selected step to find the correct exposure time. If the desired image tone would fall between two steps, average their times.

Setup for making a test strip from a single strip of film. The film is put on a two-inch strip of enlarging paper, which is resting on a sponge-rubber pad, and is then covered with a heavy, laminated plate of glass to assure good contact. As test exposures are made, the film is progressively covered up with a sheet of cardboard.

Setup for contacting a whole roll of film (seven strips) on a single sheet of 8×10 enlarging paper (the cover glass is still propped up behind the sponge-rubber pad).

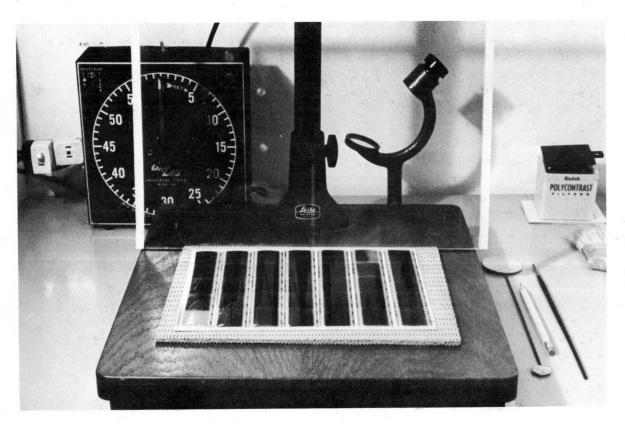

Now expose a contact using a full sheet of paper and a whole roll of film. It is a good idea to have all the strips in their original order and right side up, for this will make it easier to work with them later. Using the time obtained from the test strip, make an exposure, then process the contact.

● Processing Contacts and Enlargements

Contacts and enlargements should be handled in exactly the same way and with the same care, so the processing instructions for both will be given in this section. Some people tend to get sloppy when making contacts, but this is not good. A poorly exposed and processed contact is an offense to the aesthetic sense, which is bad for the morale. Furthermore, there is no way of extracting from it accurate information of either a technical or a pictorial nature. So heed this advice: always make the best possible contacts; if one of them doesn't come out quite right, make it over again.

Development: With a single movement, push the exposed print face down into the developer, push it around a few times, then turn it face up. Keeping it shoved under the surface, continue to move it around in the developer in a random pattern. Do this by nudging it with the tips of your fingers (or print tongs) or by lifting up the tray from different sides at random. Do not hold onto the print, because the heat from your fingers will make the developer around them more active, causing ugly brown stains.

At around 68 F the normal developing-time range for most printing papers is from 1¼ to 2¼ minutes. If a print has to be removed from the tray in less time it is definitely overexposed and should be remade. Having to develop longer than 2¼ minutes indicates definite underexposure. However, a print can sometimes be pushed to three, four, or five minutes with good results, but such extended overdevelopment *may* cause fog, stain, or mottle. You just have to try it and see. Of course, a print may be so seriously underexposed that *no* amount of time will help it.

Sometimes, and with some brands of paper, you can safely go as low as thirty to forty-five seconds, but it is not usually recommended. In such a short time, prints tend to look very mottled and muddy unless your agitation technique is superb or they are presoaked in water before development. Even then they may look bad. There is also a definite loss of image contrast (which may or may not be desirable with a given picture), and the blacks are usually not very black.

One problem with using abnormally short developing times is that you may not notice serious image degradation until your prints are dry, when it is too late to remake them easily. Just to be safe, then, remake any prints (including contacts!) that develop in less than 1¼ minutes.

Many teachers insist that their students work in a 2–2¼-minute time range, saying that this will give them the best "print quality." Any print that does not develop within that range should be automatically remade, they say. Though it is a very good discipline it goes just a bit too far. On the other hand, many really fabulous printers stick closely to this schedule.

If the developer temperature goes above 68 degrees (which is considered the ideal), cut all the times somewhat. If it is around 60 or 65, increase them. However, at 60 and below, only a heavily overexposed print will develop in a reasonable amount of time, and print quality may suffer considerably. Thus it is better to warm up the developer with the plastic-bag trick from the preceding chapter. Or you can wrap a heating pad in plastic and put it under the developer tray, turning it on from time to time.

While a print is developing do not hold it close to the safelight to examine it, because safelights are only *relatively* safe and will cause fog if too close. Using a larger than recommended bulb in a safelight will also cause fog. Of course, you would like to see the print better, but in time you will learn to judge its quality while it remains in the developer tray.

When a print has developed fully, lift it from

33

the developer tray by one corner and let it drain about five seconds, so that you limit the amount of developer being transferred to the stop bath. Then put it into the stop bath.

Stop bath: Constantly agitate the print for the first five to ten seconds, then leave it in the bath for a total of about thirty seconds, agitating intermittently. This bath not only acidifies your print but quickly stops its development, because the developer remaining in the emulsion and paper base can work only when it is in an alkaline state.

There is an impatient tendency to rush prints through the stop bath and into the hypo so that they can be examined under white light as soon as possible. Not so good. Remember that the function of the stop bath is to protect the hypo from the developer's alkalinity. By rushing, you will lose the protection and shorten the effective life of the hypo as much as 75 per cent or more. However, for resin-coated (RC) papers, five seconds is enough time in the stop bath.

First hypo: Agitate constantly for the first ten seconds, then briefly every thirty seconds or so. Leave regular paper in the tray from three to five minutes, resin-coated (RC) paper one minute.

Do not let prints overlap in the hypo, especially if it is fresh. It has a slight bleaching action, so the overlapping will cause obvious tonal demarcations across the prints underneath. Because of this bleaching effect you should use the shorter time with fresh hypo, gradually extending it as more and more prints are run through it. The time for RC papers should stay at one minute. However, *no* paper should fix *longer* than the suggested time in either hypo bath, unless you have prints that are too dark and in need of bleaching.

After the time is up, drain the print for about five seconds and put it into the next hypo bath.

Second hypo: Again, agitate constantly for the first ten seconds and intermittently thereafter. The total time is three to five minutes for regular paper, one for RC. When the time is up, immediately drain the print and put it in the "water holding bath" (the tray with water in it). Agitate it

there for a few seconds, too, then leave it in the water until you are ready to wash it.

The "hypo light": For accurately judging print exposure, contrast, and general quality it is good to have a white light positioned right over the hypo tray. A 150-watt bulb at a distance of three feet is about right. If the bulb is too small you will find yourself accepting prints that are actually underexposed quite a bit, while with too large a one you'll like overexposed pictures.

Print washing: Unless you use a washing aid such as Perma Wash your prints should wash for an hour in rapidly running water, even if you use the two-bath hypo system. Ideal water temperatures: 65–75 F for ordinary paper, 65–70 for RC. If you use a tray and tray siphon there should be at least twelve changes of water during the hour. To test how long it takes to make a complete change, remove the prints from the tray and drop in a few drops of food coloring; it should disappear completely within five minutes.

As an alternative to a tray you can use the bathtub, steadily filling it up and draining it, refilling it and draining, until the time is up.

With either method you should frequently agitate by pulling prints up from the bottom and putting them on top. *Constant* agitation would be even better, though very tedious.

According to the Heico chemists, with Perma Wash you can get the equivalent of an hour's ordinary wash with just a two-minute first wash, a two-minute Perma Wash bath, and a two-minute final wash. Just in case your washing techniques are a little sloppy or you are washing a lot of prints at one time, increase all the suggested times to five minutes each—which Heico says will give you the equivalent of a six-hour plain-water wash. Whichever times you use, the agitation should be constant throughout the entire process, and there should be a rapid flow of water during the washes. As you see, even with five-minute intervals you can save yourself forty-five minutes—at a time when one is usually worn out from printing.

If you use resin-coated (RC) paper you won't

need Perma Wash, however, because a four-minute ordinary wash in rapidly running water, with constant agitation, will do the job very well. The reason is that an RC emulsion is coated on plastic instead of paper. Plastic doesn't absorb hypo, and washing it out of a thin emulsion is fairly easy. However, hypo clings tenaciously to paper, making it necessary to use washing aids or to wash prints for a tediously long time. One of the main reasons for the introduction of RC was to nearly eliminate this tedium.

For all the welcome wonders of RC paper it would be a good idea to double the recommended wash time, especially if you are washing quite a few prints at once. The problem is that hypo tends to get between them, even with constant agitation, and that it takes a little time to wash it out.

Print drying: Perhaps the easiest way to dry prints made on regular printing paper is to wipe off both sides with an ordinary sponge and put them between sheets of photographic blotter paper. Blotter rolls and books aren't so good, because the lint they sometimes leave on prints is very hard to remove. Don't put your prints in telephone books, magazines, newspapers, and the like, for they all contain hypo as a paper preservative; and that is the very chemical we are trying to get rid of.

You can stack up your blotters, but not too many at once, because that will slow up drying considerably. If you lay a stack out flat the prints will tend to curl in every direction as they dry. To prevent this, prop up two opposite ends of the blotters on boxes or piles of books, so that they curve gently. Then your dried prints will curl in the same uncomplicated, easy-to-handle way.

If you have steam heat or live in an arid climate your prints may curl like steel springs no matter how you dry them, which is terribly exasperating. To counteract the curl, soak prints in a "print-flattening agent" just before drying them. This chemical helps the paper base retain some of its moisture, thus taking much of the spring out of it.

Drying is even simpler with resin-coated (RC) papers. You merely sponge them off and lay them face up on blotters, a bedspread, a clean table top, towels or sheets from the laundry hamper, or a clean stretch of the floor. It is not necessary to put anything on top of them; and in a short while they will be dry. Though they may get a little springy in very dry air it's not too bad. And they curl in just one direction.

● The Two-Bath Hypo System

You have seen that all the basic information on exposing and processing prints has been included in this chapter on contacts, because contacts and enlargements should be handled in exactly the same way. Now is also an appropriate time to explain why we use two hypo baths instead of just one. Indeed, many people *do* use just one, so you ought to know what difference it makes.

Remember that hypo changes unexposed silver halides into hypo-silver compounds not sensitive to light, so that they won't turn your pictures black. These new compounds are also water-soluble and can be eliminated from prints by washing, which is very necessary. Left in your prints, they would eventually bleach them or turn them brown, especially under conditions of high heat and humidity.

Unfortunately, these hypo-silver salts are only *relatively* soluble, which explains why, even with a two-bath system, a print should be washed a whole hour—unless a washing aid is used. It is especially hard to remove them from a paper base. Furthermore, the longer a given hypo bath is used the less soluble are the hypo-silver salts formed in it, until we eventually reach a point where even days or weeks of washing won't get rid of them. This dooms the pictures to eventual chemical destruction.

One solution is to use a single hypo bath, run just a few prints through it, then mix a fresh bath. But this would be inconvenient and expensive. A better method is the two-bath system, which is convenient, effective, and economical.

The first bath thoroughly desensitizes the print and forms the water-soluble compounds in the emulsion and paper base. With extended use of the bath, however, they become less and less soluble.

Since it has relatively little work to do, the second bath stays quite fresh and solves the solubility problem with ease. It converts the nearly insoluble salts already formed into relatively soluble ones, so that they can be eliminated by washing. Even so, the washing times already given should be followed closely, because they are based on the assumption that a two-bath system is being used. With an inefficient fixation system, we might have to extend the times from minutes to hours.

Eventually, the chemical energy of both hypo baths will be used up, but the first bath will go first because it takes the brunt of the work. So we discard it first and move the second hypo tray into its place in the processing line. Then we mix a *fresh* second hypo as a replacement. But how do we know when to shift trays?

According to Eastman Kodak, you can run two hundred regular 8×10 prints, or 350 RC prints, through the system before shifting and remixing—with trays that contain one gallon each. For smaller trays we would cut the figures proportionally. After four of these shifts, things begin to catch up with us and we have to start from scratch again with *both* baths freshly mixed.

Undoubtedly, the Kodak figures are based on using the stop bath with maximum efficiency, which means remixing it every time it starts to turn purple, leaving prints in it a long enough time, and agitating them thoroughly. There is no problem with resin-coated (RC) papers, which need only five seconds, but the thirty-second wait with regular papers will seem tedious to some people.

A reasonable compromise between impatience and impeccable technique is to process only one hundred regular prints, or 175 RC's, before shifting trays and remixing. Do this only for insurance, however, not to encourage yourself to use sloppy technique. If you are careless enough in your use of the stop bath you can easily knock out your two-bath hypo system long before you have put even one hundred regular (175 RC) prints through it. Indeed, you can ruin it in a single printing session. And you may not even realize what you have done. In fact, you may not discover your mistake (in the form of brown or faded prints) for months or years, but it will certainly confront you· eventually. So please look ahead!

• Note Keeping

We have covered the basic information on exposure and processing and can now return to contacts per se. Assuming that the first roll you contact was normally exposed and developed, it shouldn't be necessary to go through the whole test-strip procedure with the rolls to follow. Use the same data. While you are making your first contact, keep a record as follows:

Negatives: normally exposed and developed
Paper: Kodabrome (RC), medium contrast
Enlarger position: top of standard
Aperture: stopped down two
Time: twelve seconds

When you contact rolls that are underexposed (too light) or overexposed (too dark) you have to use test strips to get different exposures, which you can add to your list for use in the future with similar rolls. Since making contacts is a bit of a drag, you might as well do it the easiest possible way, which is to work from notes.

• Dodged Contacts

Occasionally you will have a roll in which some of the five-frame strips (35-mm) are considerably lighter or darker than the rest, so that they look rather bad on a contact. Thus there is no way of telling whether they are worth enlarging, though they actually might make very good prints. However, they can be made to look very good on the contact by dodging and burning-in during exposure (pages 71ff.). To make it very easy to do, position the improperly exposed strips at the bottom of the printing paper and all the normal strips above them.

When only one or two isolated frames are off, however, it is easier to contact-print them individually on small chips of paper. When they have been washed and dried, trim them with scissors and glue them in their proper places on the front of the large contact. Elmer's Glue works fine.

● Marking Up Contacts

With a bright enough hypo light you can analyze a contact fairly well as soon as it has been thoroughly fixed, but for evaluation in depth it is necessary to wait until it has been washed and dried. Then you can go over it centimeter by centimeter with a magnifier—the stronger the better —and use a china marker to make notes and diagrams on it for later use.

The primary function of a contact is to help you decide whether you have actually accomplished anything on a given roll. With the magnifier you can see if the images are sharp, analyze their composition, check the expressions and poses of models, evaluate lighting patterns, look for extraneous things in pictures, and so on. While you are doing this you have an opportunity to thoroughly assess your feelings about the pictures and pick the ones you really feel like enlarging. You may choose a few for immediate enlargement, put aside others until you are in the proper mood for printing them, and decide to do nothing further with the majority.

Since rejecting your own pictures is discouraging, you will find it enheartening to hear that a professional photographer considers himself very lucky if he gets even two good pictures on a roll and is quite used to getting rolls with none at all. In this perspective you see that you shouldn't ask too much of yourself, especially in the beginning.

If you had no contact to guide you, you would probably find yourself enlarging most of the pic-

tures on a roll just to get an idea of what they look like. This is a serious waste of time, effort, and printing paper. Furthermore, people who put a lot of work into the wrong pictures usually start lying to themselves, trying very hard to believe they like them when they actually do not. However, they eventually force themselves to reject them, often motivated by adverse responses from other people. This is a much greater agony than rejecting a tiny image on a contact sheet, you may be sure. Since giving up deficient images is an everyday part of photography, you should do it in the easiest way. Bear in mind that there is no photographer in the world who can get a winner in every frame.

Another thing to consider is that looking at contacts is in many ways as great a pleasure as looking at enlargements, which is a good excuse for not feeling compelled to enlarge them all. If they are pleasing already, why gild the lily? This explains why you were asked to always make the best possible contacts: so that you can enjoy them more. Conversely, there are few things more disheartening to photographers than sloppy contact sheets.

To "mark up" a contact simply means to draw on it with a china marker, usually red because of its high visibility. With a magnifier under a bright light you can see the little images very well, so you make penciled notes to guide you when you are working under the dim illumination of safelights. Mainly, you indicate the frames you wish to enlarge and how you wish to "crop" them. Cropping means to print less than the whole image, the excess being blocked off by the edges of the printing easel. Without pencil notes and diagrams for guidance you would frequently find yourself enlarging the wrong frames or using croppings that don't work very well.

Since there is no special style used in marking up, you can do it in any way that suits your fancy and helps you remember the decisions you have made with respect to printing the frames. It would be wise to do it neatly, however, as there is no point in offending your aesthetic sense. For neatest results, sharpen the china marker with a razor blade and use a ruler or a strip of cardboard for drawing lines. Mistakes in drawing or marking up the wrong frame can easily be removed with lighter fluid and a piece of cloth or cotton.

At this point you should see that there is nothing difficult or mysterious about marking up contacts. You merely examine the images in detail, make decisions concerning how you wish to enlarge them, then record the decisions on the contacts in the form of lines and little notes to yourself.

• Evaluating the Exposure of Negatives

A contact can tell you whether your negatives are overexposed, normal, or underexposed. You can't always determine this from the pictorial quality of the contact, however, for all three types will make pleasant little pictures if the contact itself is properly exposed and developed. Unfortunately, this can lead one to enlarge images that aren't technically adequate. For example, badly underexposed negatives will sometimes make very handsome contacts, but there is little chance of making fine enlargements from them. Misled, one enlarges them anyway.

To circumvent this illusory promise of good enlargement quality, examine the areas of printing paper between the strips, not the images themselves. Look also at the film borders around the images. Assuming that the contact has been well made, the in-between areas will look dark (but not quite black) if the negatives were normally exposed. The borders of the film itself will look dark gray.

If the negatives were underexposed, these areas in between strips will be medium to light gray and the film borders even lighter. Though the little pictures may look fine it will be nearly impossible to make good enlargements from them.

With overexposed negatives the in-between areas *and* the borders will probably look black. On the borders we find frame numbers and the name of the film, which are repeated every few inches. The numbers and letters will tend to be "blocked up." That is, the surrounding silver "bleeds" into them, making them look ragged or obliterating them entirely. Such negatives will usually make enlargements that are only barely acceptable because of coarse grain and fuzziness.

• Evaluating Negative Contrast

How well one likes a picture depends to a considerable degree on its contrast, so we have explored controls for contrast in negatives, prints, and pictorial subjects themselves.

With photographic subjects the main control is lighting, which may be contrasty, medium, or flat. However, they may also have inherent contrast, for instance a white building with a black roof.

With negatives, the controls are exposure, the contrast of the subject, the inherent contrast of a given film (which can vary greatly from type to type), the activity of a given developer (which can also vary a lot), the relative freshness of the developer, its temperature, agitation, and the developing time.

Assuming that you intend to use only the recommended films, all medium-contrast, and D-76, a medium-contrast developer, the number of contrast controls is reduced somewhat. Ordinarily, one works for medium-contrast negatives, though this is not always true. Nevertheless, the following tables assume that deviation from the average is not desirable, for this is usually the case.

A marked-up contact sheet. You make little notes and reminders to yourself in this manner. Since there are no rules for it, you can do it in any way you like.

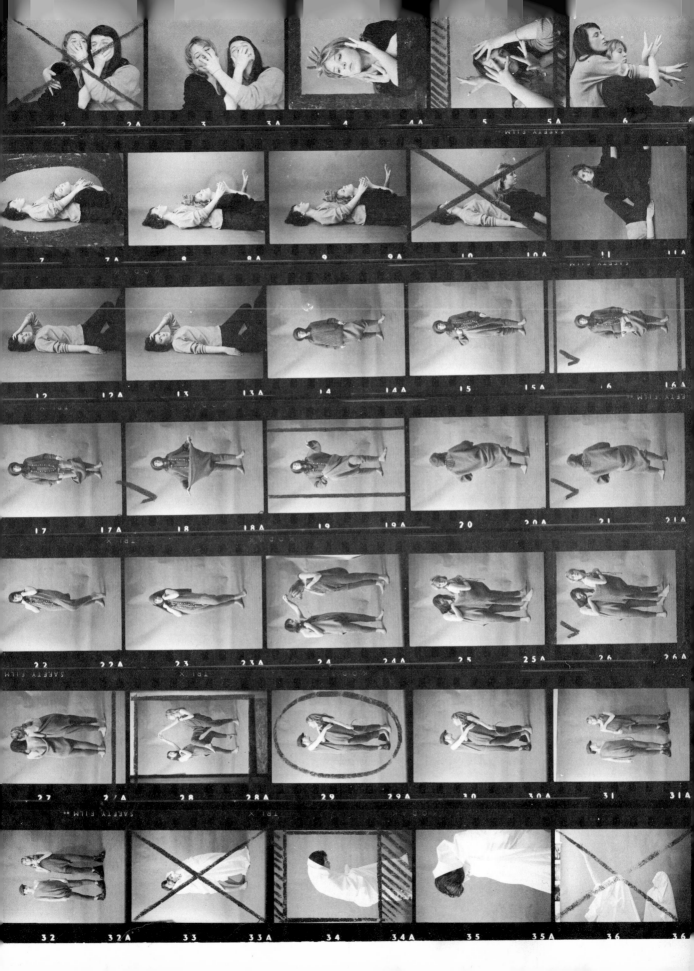

Reasons for negatives with too much contrast:

Contrasty pictorial subject matter
Processing too soon after mixing the developer
   from the dry chemical
Forgetting to dilute the developer stock solution
Too much agitation
Too high a developer temperature
Too long a developing time

Reasons for negatives with too little contrast:

Subject matter with little contrast
Underexposure
Using a chemically contaminated developer
Using an exhausted developer
Using a developer that has been stored too long
   after being mixed from the dry chemical
Diluting the developer stock solution too much
Too little agitation
Too low a developer temperature
Too short a developing time

If you wish to deliberately manipulate negative contrast it is best to change only the exposure and developing time, following the rules for everything else. For a considerable drop in contrast, try quadrupling the exposure of your negatives and cutting the developing time in half. To increase it, use a normal exposure, but increase the developing time 50 per cent. The only way to decide what these procedures can do for you is to try them, which is easy.

In printing, our contrast controls are fewer, the main one being papers with different degrees of contrast built into them. Printing papers are "graded," with numbers running from 1 (low contrast) through 6 (very high). A no. 1 would be used for a contrasty negative, a no. 6 for a very flat one. Grades 2 and 3 are considered "normal"; a "normal negative" should fit either one or the other. However, one can get excellent prints from negatives that don't fit them.

There are also "variable-contrast" papers, with four different contrast grades inherent in them. By using different-colored "printing filters" under the enlarger lens one can get grades 1 through 4 from a single package of paper. When you have to buy only one package of paper instead of four you can buy it in one-hundred-sheet boxes and save quite a bit of money per sheet. There is also no danger of running out of any of the grades while you have any paper left at all.

When printing contacts, we use a paper of a slightly lower grade than usual, a no. 2 being considered normal, as are any negatives that contact well on it. The reason is that the smaller an image is the more contrast it has. Thus a normal negative that would look good on no. 2 in a contact might require a no. 3 paper for an 8×10 enlargement and a no. 4 for a large blow-up.

With this perspective, if you find yourself contacting on no. 3 you will know that your negatives are a bit flat. A no. 4 indicates they are not so good but probably still passable. If you have to go all the way to a 5 or 6 they are very flat indeed and will be difficult or impossible to enlarge handsomely. However, if you have to use a no. 1 paper or filter you are in no trouble, for there are several good ways of reducing print contrast. Furthermore, you probably won't even need them, unless the contact on no. 1 looks very contrasty.

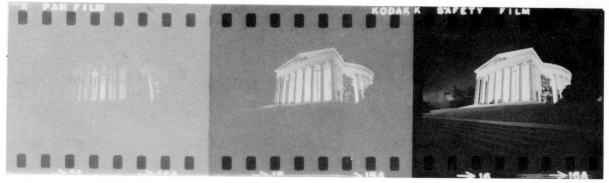

A   B   C

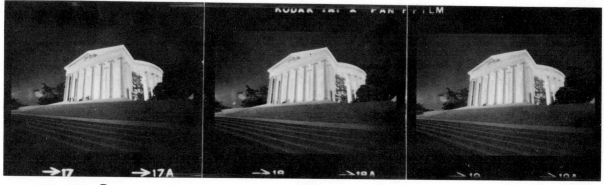

D   E   F

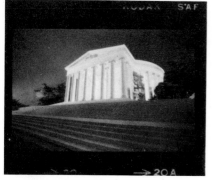

G

Individual contact prints made from a series of negatives with different exposures. adjacent prints having exposures exactly one stop apart. Negative D is the normal exposure. Thus C, B, and A are progressively one, two, and three stops underexposed. E, F, and G are progressively one, two, and three stops overexposed. Note that the overexposed negatives make better images than the underexposed ones. Note also that the film border prints gradually darker as we move from underexposure to overexposure. For the normal negative it prints dark gray, not black, though the surrounding paper is almost black. As we move toward heavy overexposure the tonal difference between the film border and the surrounding paper disappears. By examining contacts in this manner you can tell if your negatives were properly exposed, or in what direction they deviate from the normal.

print A

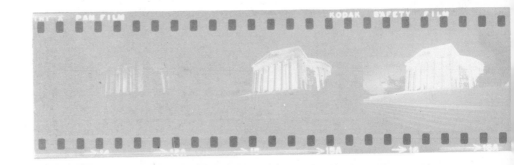

print B

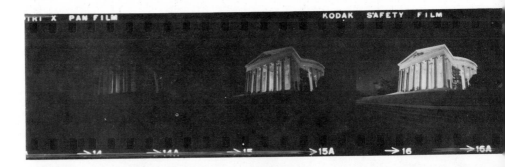

print C

A strip of negatives one stop apart in exposure was contact-printed in three different ways. Contact print A was exposed to make the thinnest negative (on the far left of the strip) reproduce as well as possible and thus had a very short printing exposure time. Print B, with a longer time, was printed for the normal negative in the center of the negative strip. Print C, with a very long exposure, was printed for the negative on the far right end öf the strip. This negative was three stops overexposed.

This chart suggests what can happen on any contact sheet if the negative exposures vary considerably from one another. Some pictures will come out too

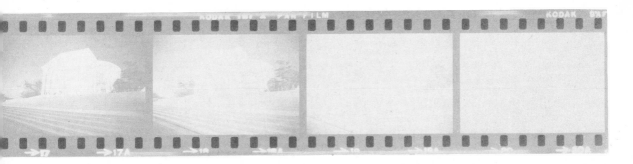

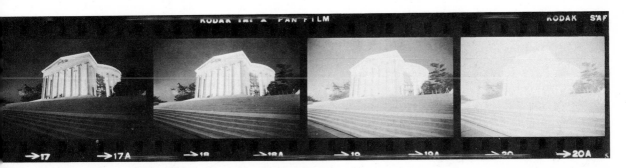

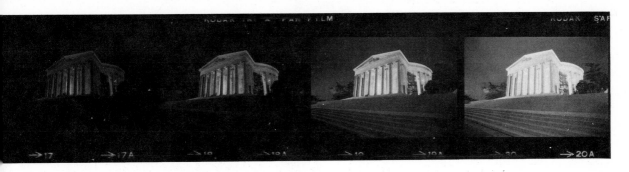

light, some just right, and some too dark. You can't
really tell how the too light and too dark ones will look
when enlarged. The only way you can tell is to make
several contact sheets with different printing exposure
times. None of these single-strip contact prints (A, B,
and C) can by itself tell us which of the negatives are
actually printable, but the three together tell us quite a
bit. Now think of the original negative strip from
which these contacts were made: The five negatives on
the bottom right would all make passable prints, though
the enlarged prints from the two on the far right would
be quite grainy. The remaining negatives would make
very poor prints.

HOW TO CLEAN NEGATIVES AND
MAKE MINOR REPAIRS
NEGATIVE DEFECTS AND THEIR CAUSES

Unless a negative is carefully cleaned just before it is put in the enlarger, the minute specks of dust and lint that cling to the back of it are likely to produce unsightly white spots and lines on the print. Though such defects can be removed from the print by retouching ("spotting"), it can be very hard and tedious work if there are a lot of them. Thus the best thing to do is to prevent them by using adequate negative-cleaning methods. However, there are things other than dust and lint that make for messy prints. They may originate in the film cassette, the camera, or the enlarger—or they may be due to faulty film processing, drying, and handling. They, too, can be prevented. If through carelessness you should get these negative defects, they can usually (but not always) be repaired or compensated for.

● Clean Negatives Just Before Printing

Using one or more of the methods that follow, you should clean each negative *just before* putting it in the enlarger. You may have to repeat a procedure several times in order to get a given negative clean enough. If you wish to temporarily

remove it from the enlarger, clean it *again* before putting it back. This is not overdoing it, though it may seem so. It happens that in only a second or two a cleaned negative can pick up a fresh load of dust or lint.

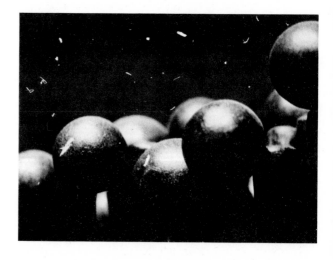

An enlargement made from a very dirty negative. It would be a long and tedious job to fill in the spots with spotting dye.

• Static Electricity

The main problem is that the back of a negative (but not the emulsion) can readily pick up a charge of static electricity, so that like a strong magnet it will attract dust from the air, even from a distance of several inches. It also holds onto the dust when you are trying to get rid of it. We have this static problem often enough at normal room temperatures, but in a cold and dry darkroom it becomes infinitely worse.

The static charge explains why negatives can get dirty without being touched and why they should be put into the enlarger *immediately* after cleaning. The use of the anti-static materials on our list will remove the charge when used properly. Though dust will still be somewhat of a problem the negatives will at least not be attracting it magnetically.

• Dust Is the Enemy

Whether you are drying freshly developed film or making prints, dust in the air will cause you lots of trouble—and there is always more of it than you think. So don't stir up more of it. Don't sweep your darkroom just before starting to work, because it will fill the air with dust particles for an hour or more. So will moving equipment and materials around too vigorously. Do your cleaning the day before, preferably with a vacuum cleaner. Instead of brushing off work surfaces, wipe them with a damp sponge. Clean your enlarger and enlarger table in the same way. On the lens and condenser use lens tissue, however, for it will not scratch their delicate surfaces. If the air in your darkroom is already filled with dust, sprinkle the floor liberally with water, then go elsewhere for an hour or two. The water will pick up much of the dust.

• Materials for Negative Cleaning and Minor Repair

It is highly unlikely that you will need all the things on this list, but it is good to know about them in case you ever do. Most of the time, you can get along very well with just the sable brush, the nose grease, and the silicone cloth.

A no. 4, pointed sable (not camel-hair) brush
Nose grease
A silicone anti-static negative- or record-cleaning cloth
Marshall's Film Klens, or a similar anti-static film cleaner
A clean, well-worn handkerchief or other soft cloth
Vaseline
Surgical cotton
Q-Tips
Dektol, stop bath, and hypo
Kodak black opaque
Round toothpicks
An artist's crow-quill pen
No. 2 and 2-H pencils
Rubbing alcohol
Lighter fluid
The finest emery cloth (purple)
Hand soap

• Checking for Dust

If you have processed your negatives properly, dried them in a clean place, and stored them individually in five-frame lengths (35-mm) in glassine sleeves, your cleaning problems will be minimal and the simplest cleaning methods entirely adequate. There will be no need for making repairs.

Before cleaning a negative you need a way of telling if it has dust or lint on it. Particles that will make a mess of a print may be so small that you can't see them at all in ordinary light. One way to make them stand out is to turn on the enlarger light, open up the lens all the way, and hold the negative up close to it at right angles. Then even the tiniest particles will be visible. You should make this check both before and after cleaning.

An even better method requires a kind of enlarger in which the lamp housing rests on the negative carrier and can be lifted up or tilted back. You put the cleaned negative and carrier in it and turn on the light before lowering the housing. Looking across the negative at right angles, you can easily see any dust or lint that you may have missed.

● Brush and Nose Grease

When using either checking method, one can easily pick off dust and lint particles with the sable brush, provided the negative doesn't have too high a static charge. Ordinarily, the brush would drop as much dust as it would pick up, but we use a minute amount of grease to make the dust stick to it.

To lightly grease your brush, stroke it two or three times in the oily crease at the side of your nostril. Don't use Vaseline, because you would certainly overdo it. The "nose grease system" has been popular with professional printers for years, so you don't have to look askance at it.

With either checking system some grease will be visible on the negative but won't show up on prints, because there is actually very little of it. Frequently, the brush alone will do a very adequate cleaning job, as will the following basic method.

● Thumb-and-Finger Method

On your left hand, vigorously rub together the ball of your thumb and the side of your index finger to dislodge any dust or lint on them. Then put a strip of negatives between them, with the shiny side (back) facing your thumb. While maintaining gentle pressure with finger and thumb, pull the strip slowly through with the other hand. Repeat this process two or three times. Of course, your hands should be clean and

By raising the enlarger head and turning on the light, you can see dust on the back of a negative. Then you can pick it all off with a sable brush that has a little nose grease in it.

One good way to clean a strip of negatives is to draw it gently between the ball of the thumb and the side of the index finger. The back of the strip should face the thumb. Your hands should be very clean and dry.

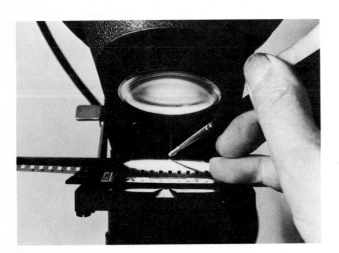

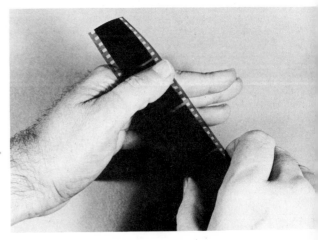

dry, or you may damage your negative. This is another old-time professional trick, and a very good one.

• Anti-static Methods

Unfortunately, neither the brush nor the finger method is very effective when used alone if a negative is highly charged. In this case one should try an anti-static cloth or spray. To use the cloth, shake it out or brush it off vigorously, to make sure there is no abrasive grit on it. Now fold it once and draw the *whole strip* through the fold, using gentle pressure. Do this two or three times. Wiping off only the frame you wish to print may not remove the charge at all, whereas the whole-strip method will remove both the static and the dust.

Unfortunately, the available anti-static cloths are so poorly made that they leave their own lint on negatives when one uses them. However, with the static charge gone the lint can be easily removed with the brush. Though this lint problem

The splotches on this print were caused by dirty rinse water, which left an oily sludge on the back of the negative. Sludge can usually be wiped off with cotton or a clean soft cloth.

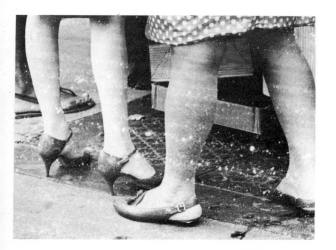

is a pain in the neck, the silicone cloth is nevertheless an excellent cleaning tool.

To use an anti-static cleaner like Marshall's, spray the entire strip of negatives on both sides, then gently wipe them off with a soft lintless cloth. Be sure the cloth has no dust or grit on it, for they can scratch negatives with ease. Take care not to inhale the Marshall's or get it in your eyes, because it contains isopropanol, which can adversely affect the heart, liver, and eye membranes. After cleaning, give the selected frame a final check and pick off any dust with the brush. If you find that dust clings to your enlarger and negative carrier it means that they are electrically charged, too. Spray them with Marshall's, then leave the room until the smell had dissipated.

• Oily Sludge

The foregoing methods should take care of your cleaning problems about 99 per cent of the time, yet you will occasionally need other techniques, too. For example, we sometimes have trouble from a very thin coating of oily sludge on the film backing (but never the emulsion). It causes a mottled effect in prints, especially if the negatives are "thin" (underexposed and/or underdeveloped). The sludge comes from the wash or final Photo-Flo rinse water, having gotten into the water pipes from a usually unknown source. Fortunately, one can gently wipe it off a negative with a soft dry cloth or cotton wool. In the unlikely event that it resists cleaning we can soak the cloth or cotton wool in lighter fluid or rubbing alcohol.

• Chewing Gum and What Not

Now and then we encounter such unlikely problems as chewing gum, the sticky coatings from masking or adhesive tape, grease, syrup, coffee, or Lord knows what. There seems to be an infinity of ways of messing up negatives when people are really determined to do it. Or when non-photographer members of the family, especially children, start handling negatives without permission. Fortunately, we have several types of solvents: water, soap and water, lighter fluid, and rubbing alcohol. Alone or together, they will take care of most problems of this sort.

• Embedded Dirt

Embedded dust is considerably harder to deal with than loose dust or lint. It gets tightly embedded in the emulsion when film is dried in a dusty room. If the emulsion is also softer than it should be, there will be even more embedded dirt. This undue softness can be caused by washing film too long. Or an overused fixer can be the culprit, because the hardener component in it may be used up, or exhausted. Ordinarily, a film emulsion is very soft all the way through processing, until it is hardened by the fixer, but with a worn-out fixer it may never get hardened at all. Too short a time in a good fixer could be the cause, as could washing in warm water.

The cure for embedded dirt may seem a bit strange, but it works well if you are patient and extremely careful. Otherwise it is an invitation to disaster. Put the negative in a clean tray of fresh print developer, handling it only by the edges. We are using the developer only for the alkali that it contains; it will thoroughly soften the emulsion in a minute or so. Let it get quite soft.

Now take a loose swatch of cotton about the size of a golf ball and get it sopping wet in the developer. Leaving the negative at the bottom of the developer (which should be about one half inch deep), gently drag the loose cotton back and forth along the strip until the dirt has been dislodged. Remember that the emulsion is *very* soft. Don't get impatient and start *rubbing,* because the dust particles, and the cotton itself, will act as abrasives and totally ruin your negative.

After this treatment, put the film in a stop bath for a few seconds, then into hypo for five to ten minutes, where it will be hardened again. Then wash and dry it in the usual way.

Don't worry: the developer won't darken the image, because there is nothing left in the emul-sion that can develop. And there is nothing left for the fixer to fix—but the hardener component will harden the emulsion, which is all we want.

• Backing Scratches

Sometimes you will see scratch-like white lines on your prints. Indeed, they come from actual scratches on the backs of negatives. Fine and delicate though they may be, they show up on prints anyway. There are two kinds of backing scratches: straight lines running parallel to the edges of the film; and lines, either straight or curved, crossing the film in random directions.

The parallel scratches are usually caused by grit in the felt-lined slot of a film cassette, a dirty or badly designed "bulk film loader," rough spots on the camera pressure plate, or by rolling up negatives and cinching the roll tighter.

You can easily get grit in the slot by unwrapping the cassette and putting it in a pocket or camera bag instead of directly into your camera, which is the only wise thing to do. Pockets and bags are always dirtier than you think. You can use bulk loaders for 100-foot rolls of film, which you can then load into the cassette yourself. Film is much cheaper this way. However, clean or dirty, bulk loaders are prone to cause scratches—so don't use them. Ruining negatives is a poor way of economizing, don't you think?

The rectangular pressure plate is at the back of the camera and has a little spring behind it so that it can press the film flat against the film gate, which will give us pictures that are sharp from edge to edge. If its edges are a little rough they will scratch film as it is dragged across them while it is being advanced. With the finest emery cloth, smooth up any rough edges that you find.

There are a good many ways for getting random scratches on negatives, which are terribly prone to damage, anyway. Cleaning them too roughly is one way. Storing more than one in a single glassine envelope is another. A very common way of getting scratches is to pull a strip of negatives through the negative carrier while it is

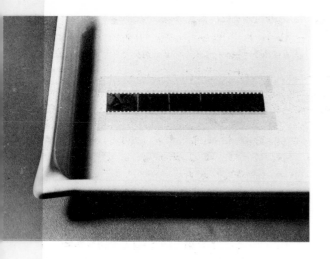

To prepare a negative for removing embedded dirt (or to bleach or intensify it—see Appendix), tape it to the bottom of a dry tray, emulsion side up, then rub the tape down hard with a thumbnail. If the tape doesn't want to stick to the tray, go over the surface first with lighter fluid, letting it dry before you put the tape down.

For removing embedded dirt, print developer has been poured over the taped-down negative. A sopping-wet wad of cotton is dragged *very gently* along the film after it has had time to get very soft in the developer. Rubbing with the cotton would ruin the negative. When the dirt is gone, discard the developer and pour hypo into the tray to harden the emulsion. Then wash and dry the film in the usual way.

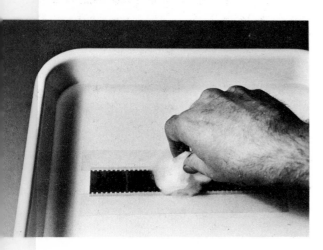

still in the enlarger. Always, one should remove the carrier, open it up, then *lift* the next frame into place.

Carrying negatives loose in pockets, purses, camera bags, or notebooks is just asking for trouble. So is letting them sit around on table tops for days. Of course, one that has been dropped on the floor and stepped on is a bad risk. We could say that the basic problem is things rubbing against negatives or negatives rubbing against things. There is *always* enough dirt around to make any rubbing whatever abrasive.

The cure for either parallel or random backing scratches is ordinary Vaseline. Remember that they make white lines on prints, which they do by scattering the enlarger light during exposure. If we could fill them in with something with about the same coefficient of refraction as the film base, they wouldn't do this. Fortunately, Vaseline fills the bill very well.

The method of application is simple. Just put a very small amount on the pad of your little finger and apply it to the back of the entire frame in small, circular patterns. What is a small amount of Vaseline? About as much as it would take to lubricate a squeaky butterfly. Not very much, you see.

Even a little Vaseline is messy, and it collects and holds dust. However, one can easily pick it off with the sable brush just before (or just after) putting the negative in the enlarger. With a thin negative, the Vaseline swirls may show up as patterns on the prints, so the Vaseline should be wiped off and a thinner coating applied. With normal or heavy (dark) negatives there is seldom any problem, unless one is using far too much Vaseline. Remember, we are only filling minute scratches, and that doesn't call for much of it.

Try not to get Vaseline on the emulsion. If you accidentally do, no harm done. Just spread it around the entire frame, then wipe it all off with a soft cloth. If there is Vaseline on only a part of the frame, it will show up on the print.

Since Vaseline is chemically inert it can be left on negatives after printing, but it is a little messy that way. Photo stores sell special "anti-scratch solutions," which are just as messy. However, they work exactly as Vaseline does and cost considerably more, so there is not much point in buying them.

• Emulsion Scratches

We don't see emulsion scratches very often, because photographic gelatin is tough and scratch-resistant when it is dry. Though it is very vulnerable when wet it is only scratched then by gross mishandling. Emulsion scratches, which print up as *black* lines, can easily be repaired if they aren't too deep. However, deep ones may be very difficult or impossible to repair—on the negative. Then we have to use bleach on the black lines on the print, which can be an extremely intricate and tedious job, which few people would enjoy.

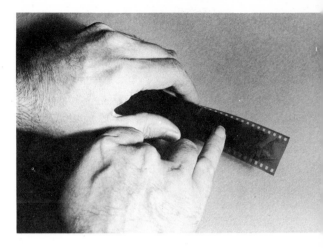

Treating a backing scratch by applying a very minute amount of Vaseline to it with the tip of the little finger.

A white line caused by a backing scratch.

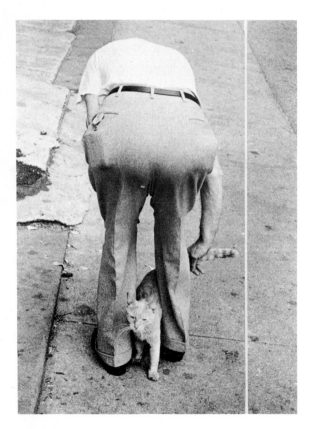

Emulsion and backing scratches are caused by the same things, except that pressure plates don't come in contact with emulsions. Instead, there may be a roughness on the camera's film gate, over which the film slides when it is advanced. Again the solution is to polish away the roughness with fine emery cloth.

Both emulsion and backing scratches are usually made when the film is dry, either before or after processing, and are characterized by sharp, clean edges. Occasionally an emulsion is scratched during processing. The soft emulsion tears or digs up like old Jell-O, giving us scratches with jagged edges all the way through the gelatin. The usual culprit: long fingernails, which chop up the film as it is being removed from the developing reel. These jagged-edge scratches are so difficult to repair that only a genuine fanatic would even try, especially on small negatives.

To repair sharp-edge emulsion scratches, make a little pile of graphite dust by rubbing a no. 2 pencil on fine emery cloth. Now, make a firm little ball of cotton about the size of a dime (or use a Q-Tip). Leave the graphite dust on the emery cloth and thoroughly rub one side of the cotton ball into it, until the fibers are black and well impregnated with the dust. Then blow off the loose particles.

Using moderate pressure, rub the blackened cotton back and forth *across* the scratch. Even if the edges are very sharp there will usually be enough "tooth" to take graphite from the cotton fibers and fill the scratch. However, the emulsion itself also has tooth and picks up graphite. Fortunately, one can easily rub it off with a clean piece of dry cotton, still working crosswise to the scratch to avoid wiping the graphite out of it.

One can't tell when a scratch has been filled to exactly the right degree by holding the negative up to a light source, light surface, or light box. They just don't work for this purpose. The only good way to tell is to make a small test strip for the area that includes the scratch. If it prints just a little light, consider yourself lucky; when you have gotten this far it is easier to retouch the print than to remove exactly the right amount of graphite from the scratch. On the other hand, if the scratch prints too dark, work on it some more. Otherwise, you will have to do a difficult bleaching job on your print.

Though only a fanatic would work on jagged emulsion scratches, you may be working on your

Dark lines caused by emulsion scratches on the negative. They can usually be filled in with powdered graphite, which you can make by rubbing a soft pencil on fine emery paper.

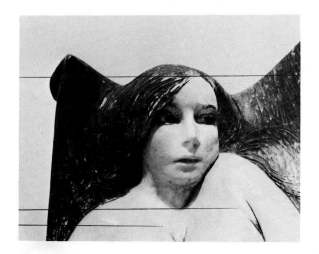

Fanatic Merit Badge. If so, try filling them in with a spotting brush and black opaque diluted with water to the consistency of ink. Or try rubbing undiluted opaque into them with a fingertip, wiping off the excess with damp cotton. There is something to be said for both systems: You can wipe off your mistakes as often as you wish without harming the negative, unless you rub on it too hard. Furthermore, the opaque has something in it that makes it stick nicely to emulsions, whereas ordinary inks and spotting colors do not.

A toothpick that has been sharpened to a needle point on emery cloth may also prove useful. Suck on it awhile to soften the point a bit, then use it for putting minute drops of very thin opaque into jagged little clear spots and torn places. For greater precision and control—but at considerable risk to your negative—you can try an artist's crow-quill pen, which has a needle-sharp point that will dig up the emulsion wherever it touches. If it touches only in the clear spots and lines you will be all right, because they will be filled with opaque, anyway.

The trick with a crow-quill is in using thin-enough opaque and getting it to feed (flow) properly. Slightly rusty or well-worn pen points work best, whereas new ones will hardly feed at all; they just won't write. The coating on the metal is the problem. Sand it off near the tip with a small piece of emery paper. It also helps if you lick the point just before sticking it in opaque. The *instant before* you intend to touch the pen to a negative you should get the flow started by writing on your thumbnail with it for a second or two. Naturally, you should practice awhile on reject negatives before digging into good ones.

Scratches and tears filled with opaque print up white, of course, which means that they have to be retouched on the print. If they fall in light image areas this is fairly easy. In medium-gray or dark areas they will drive you to the loony bin, because it takes forever to fill them in with dye. In this case, bleach on the print may prove easier than opaque in the scratch. However, some bleaching jobs are passports to the loony bin, too.

• Fuzzy, Round Blobs

Sometimes on your prints you will find round, fuzzy spots that are just a little bit lighter than the areas around them. They are caused by dirt or fingerprints on one of the lenses in the enlarger's condenser system. Breathe on the offending lens to steam it up, them wipe it clean with lens tissue. If necessary, use warm water, hand soap, and lens tissue.

• Air Bells

You may also find sharp-edged round spots on prints, but they will usually be darker than adjacent areas. Originating in the negative, they are poetically called "air bells." They are caused by faulty agitation methods during development,

Fuzzy blobs caused by dirt in the enlarger's condenser system. Cleaning these glass condensers will easily solve this problem.

which permit air bubbles to cling to the emulsion. Wherever they touch it the developer can't reach it, so no tone is built up within them. If the bubbles are there through the whole developing time, these perfectly round spots are clear, or white. If they are there for just a minute or two the spots are grayish.

If you have a sure, steady hand you can retouch fairly large air bells with a no. 2-H pencil, provided they are of the gray type, which has a little tooth. Clear types do not. Sharpen the pencil to a long, needle point on emery cloth. Then tape one end of the negative strip to a skylit window or to a light box, holding the other end away from the surface somewhat. This puts a little spring in it so the sharp pencil point won't dig in abruptly. Now, working with only the pressure permitted by this springiness, pencil in the air bell with small, circular strokes.

For air bells too small to get into with pencil you can use opaque with the pen or sharpened toothpick. However, they are not especially hard to retouch on prints, so you might as well do the repairs at the print stage. Negatives are so small nowadays that working on them with opaque is a very tricky, frustrating business, anyway.

• Other Negative Defects

The defects that have been discussed so far have all been more or less reparable. Some of the following ones are not, yet you ought to know about them anyway. Being aware of their causes will help you avoid them.

Mottle: Most easily seen in the print, which

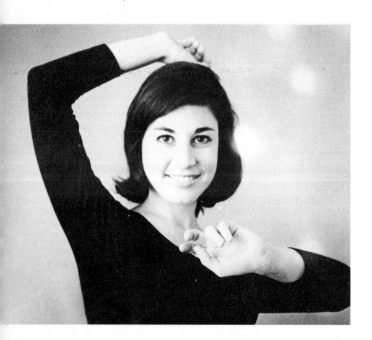

The black sun is actually on air bell that was caused by a bubble of air sticking to the film emulsion throughout the entire film-developing time. It prevented the developer from reaching the emulsion at that point, resulting in a round clear spot.

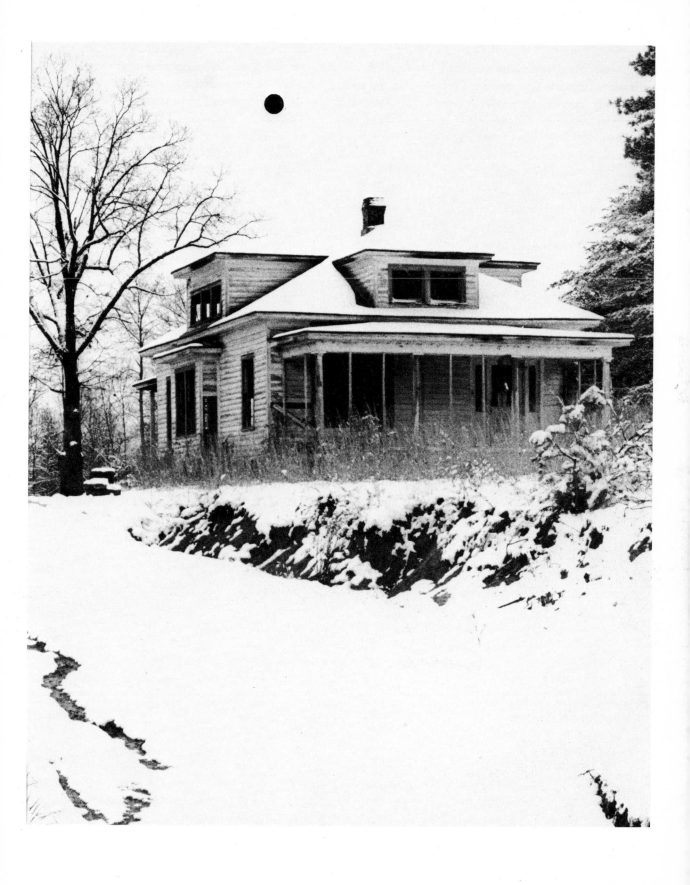

has a muddy, splotchy look. *Usual causes:* The negative was given insufficient agitation during development. May also be caused by leaving film in the developer for far too short a time. We may even get an effect that looks like a dark venetian blind. *Repair:* Both negatives and prints are usually beyond repair.

Dark edges: On a strip of negatives we see that the edge of the film is considerably darker than the center. *Usual causes:* insufficient agitation during development or using a developer that calls for too short a developing time (five minutes or less). *Repair:* on the negative, none, but dark edges can usually be corrected in printing by dodging or burning-in (pages 71ff.).

Dark streaks: Usually called "high-speed-development marks." Look for dark streaks or marks that originate on the borders of the film and go part way into the image. *Causes:* too vigorous, too frequent, or constant agitation during development. *Repair:* on the negative, none, but dark streaks can sometimes be counteracted in printing by cropping, burning-in, dodging, or retouching.

Light-struck: Dark streaks where stray light has touched the film before processing. *Usual causes:* handling film rolls or cassettes, or loading cameras, in bright sunlight; defective or worn self-load cassettes; films larger than 35-mm not wound tightly enough on their spools. *Repair:* on the negative, none, but the marks can sometimes be counteracted in printing (see "dark streaks" above).

Static marks: They usually look like black lightning flashes or fireworks displays on the negative, yet they are also found in the form of little round dots that are more or less in rows. *Causes:* Some people build up within themselves an unusual amount of static electricity, which can be discharged to unprocessed film. In cold weather or cold rooms, cameras and bulk film loaders may also build up charges if film is run through them too fast; for example, if a film advance lever or winder is used with too much vigor and haste. Some cameras and loaders are worse in this re-spect than others. *Repair:* There is nothing one can do about static marks on negatives, but the little, round ones can be retouched on prints.

Reticulation: When printed, reticulation looks like a formal tile or mosaic pattern super-imposed on all or part of the image. *Usual causes:* washing either too long or in warm water, a great temperature difference between processing solutions, or using a fixer with an exhausted hardener. *Repair:* Though it can be neither repaired nor corrected for, it is sometimes very interesting in itself.

Water marks: Irregular marks in shapes that large drops of water would make on a surface. In a print, a water spot shows up as a little area with a vaguely defined double line around it; one of the individual lines is dark, the other light. *Cause:* leaving large drops of water on the emulsion when hanging film up to dry. Last to dry, these drops pull the emulsion out of place around their peripheries, which accounts for the lines. *Repair:* Though impossible to remove from negatives, water marks can sometimes be patched up on prints.

Grain: Hard to see on negatives, grain looks like sand or granite on prints. *Causes:* overexposure, overdevelopment, developing negatives in a print developer, processing in solutions whose temperatures vary too much from one another, using an overworked fixing bath in which the hardener is exhausted, washing too long a time, and washing in warm water. Alone, any of these factors may cause grain, but it is almost a certainty if several are combined. *Repair:* There is no way of removing grain from negatives, but it can be minimized by diffusion printing or by making prints lighter than usual.

In a sense, this chapter is a long description of the woes that possibly await you, but don't let it throw you. If you carefully follow the instructions in this book, you will never in a lifetime even see most of the defects you have just read about. Remember that about 99 per cent of the time you will be able to prepare your negatives for problemless printing by using only a brush, nose grease, and a silicone cloth.

HOW TO MAKE AND USE TEST STRIPS

Making test strips is a fast, easy, and economical way to determine the correct exposure for prints. In turn, finding the right exposure is by far the most important part of the art of printing. Without test strips, one would have to take a variety of things into account, including the relative "speed" of the printing paper, the output of the enlarger bulb, the relative density of the negative, the line voltage, and so on. However, by making test strips we neatly step around such problems and yet come up with very accurate exposure information.

Test strips are so easy to make that there is a tendency to slight them. However, the information in test strips cannot be trusted unless they are carefully exposed and processed. Furthermore, they must be examined under a light that is bright enough. For more information on these matters, review the material on pages 38–40. Remember that contacts, test strips, and prints should all be treated in the same way and with great care if they are to be effective.

• Things You Need

We will again use the list given on page 27. Since it is lengthy we won't repeat it here. However, we can eliminate the glass, soap, china marker, and lighter fluid.

• Your Processing Line and Developing Procedures

Arrange your chemical trays in the way described earlier. Carefully follow the recommended processing procedures. However, you should use one specific developing time for test strips (say 1½ or two minutes), rather than use the time range from 1¼ to 2¼ minutes. We could say that either 1½ or two minutes would represent the optimum, whereas there would be a slight loss in print quality with longer or shorter times that are still within the recommended range. Since we have an accurate way for determining exposure, it only makes sense to tie it in with a developing time that will give top print quality.

In making final prints, you should also aim for a specific time. Then if you miss the correct exposure somewhat you can lengthen or shorten the time to compensate for your error. You will learn that there is a fair amount of latitude. Do not do this with test strips, however! *Always* remove them from the developer after the preselected time, even if you see that they will have to be remade.

If you violate this rule and "jerk" a test strip after, say, thirty seconds, the exposure information on it will be applicable only to a print that will also be jerked in thirty seconds. Similarly, a three-minute test strip will be applicable only to a three-minute print. Though jerking and "pushing" test strips and prints are legitimate techniques for certain purposes, they are disastrous when used in ordinary printing. So don't be lazy or impatient. As a beginner, the test strip is your best friend. Treat it with respect.

• Width of Strips

Some people get carried away with the economy idea and make test strips about one half inch wide, which is much too narrow to judge with any accuracy. An exposure that looks good on such a strip may be totally wrong for an enlargement print. A one-inch strip is usually all right, a two-inch one somewhat better. Occasionally, you should use a whole sheet of paper for a test strip —just to see what things look like—and sometimes it is the only way to get all the information you need. However, narrower strips will usually suffice.

• Placement of Strips

Since a test strip will include only a section of the image, you will naturally want exposure information concerning the most important part. For accurate placement, turn on the enlarger light and lay a pencil beside the image area you deem most important. Then turn off the light and lay the strip of paper next to the pencil.

When printing pictures of people, you usually lay the strips right across their faces. For other pictures, you kind of psych them out in trying to choose areas for which correct exposure information will be applicable to the pictures as a whole. You learn to do this through experience and experimentation.

• Exposing the Strip: the Five-Second Method

Though you were given this method earlier, it will be repeated for your convenience. Stop down the enlarger lens two or three stops. Position the strip and give *all* of it a five-second exposure.

Taking care not to push it out of place, cover up about one inch of it with a sheet of cardboard and give it another five-second exposure. Continue progressively covering it up and giving five-second exposures. On the developed strip, you can tell the exposure for a given area by counting up to it by fives from the bottom.

You usually use this method when you have an approximate idea of the range in which the correct exposure will fall, say from ten to twenty-five seconds. When you are printing a lot of negatives from the same roll, you can usually guess the range pretty well after you have printed the first one or two.

• Exposing the Strip: the 5–5–10–20 Method

This method, confusing to some, has the advantage of showing what a series of tones look like when their exposures are exactly doubled (or halved). That is, adjacent tones are one stop apart. This will help you get a better quantitative idea of what exposure does to photosensitive materials.

Setup for making a test strip with a two-inch strip of printing paper. Both ends are taped to the printing easel so that it won't shift position as the cardboard is moved across it.

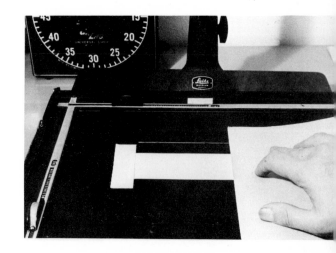

For this test, stop your lens down three or four times. As before, start by giving the whole strip an exposure, then progressively cover it up for additional exposures. However, only the *first two* exposures are alike this time. After the second one, begin progressively doubling the exposure for each succeeding step. The *individual exposures* in the series are: 5–5–10–20–40–80–160 seconds. Though you can extend the series beyond this there is usually no need to.

When we examine the developed strip we have to think of *total exposures,* which happen to add up to: 5–10–20–40–80–160–320 seconds. The exposure for a given section of a strip is its *total exposure,* not merely one of the individual exposures that were added together to make the total. Perhaps this will help you keep things straight: To tell the exposure for a particular segment, start at the bottom with 5 and count up to it by doubles: 5–10–20–etc. Or count down from 320 by halves: 320–160–80–etc. *Figure it out!*

If the *correct* exposure happens to come out long—say 80 seconds—open up two stops to make it 20. *Remember!*

An important advantage of this method is that it incorporates a much longer exposure range than the five-second system. You need this great a range when you are using unfamiliar equipment and printing materials and haven't the slightest idea where the correct exposure will fall. With a range from 5 to 320 seconds it would be hard to miss it. It will also give you a clear picture of the *tonal* range inherent in a given paper.

Many people make their test strips by uncovering the paper, though covering it is much better. Suit yourself. Warning: If you try uncovering with *this* method you will go berserk trying to figure out the total exposures.

• Remakes

There are times when it is wise to remake test strips before going on to final prints, for example when they are, all in all, either too light or too dark. This makes them relatively useless. For the light ones, open up the lens a stop or two; for the dark ones, stop down. Or you can lengthen or shorten the exposure times if you like. Since the results can be the same, do whichever is the more convenient. Remember that doubling the time is the same as opening up a stop, halving the time the same as stopping down once.

In examining a test strip, you may see that the contrast is either too high or too low for the picture. Choose another contrast of paper or printing filter and remake it. The point is that the correct exposure on one paper may be far from the correct exposure on another. In part this is because contrast and exposure depend on one another: where one varies, the other should also. Another reason is that different paper grades, or variable-contrast papers used with different filters, have different speeds, or light sensitivity. A good exposure for one paper wouldn't be right for another that is 30 per cent more sensitive to light. The general rule is: the lower the paper or filter number the greater the speed, and vice versa.

• Exposure Chips

Sometimes it is convenient to make an exposure test with a single 2×2-inch or larger chip of paper, positioning it in the most important part of the picture and making a single exposure by pure guesswork based on prior experience. Though this exposure may prove to be considerably off, one learns in time to make rather accurate exposure determinations using chips that are as much as one stop off in either direction. This is not recommended for beginners, however.

Another approach is to make two exposures on the chip, one that you estimate will be a bit too much, the other a bit too little. From analyzing the two-tone chip you can then estimate the exposure between the two that would be exactly right.

TOTAL
A   EXPOSURES   B

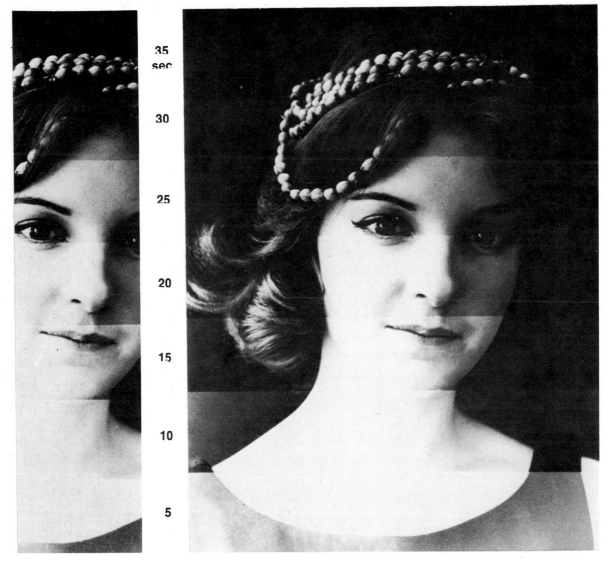

35
sec

30

25

20

15

10

5

TOTAL

C   **EXPOSURES**   **D**

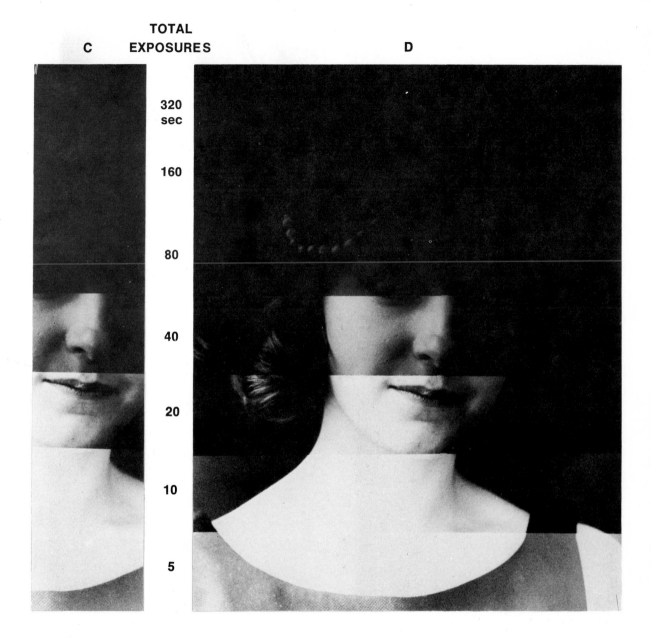

320 sec

160

80

40

20

10

5

Four test strips made from the same negative. A (two-inch) and B (full-sheet) were made with the 5–5–5–5 method (exposure increments of five seconds). C and D were made with the 5–5–10–20 system (total exposures progressively doubled). The full-sheet tests obviously give us more information than the 2-inch ones. However, the narrow ones tell us enough to permit us to successfully extrapolate from them. Note that the exposure range with the 5–5–10–20 system is much greater than with the 5–5–5–5 system.

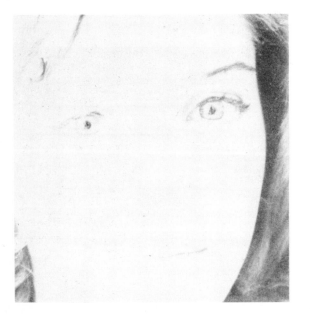

5 seconds

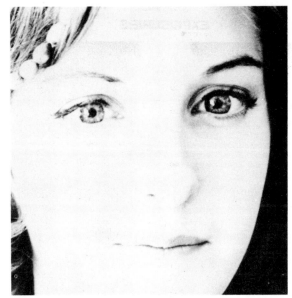

10 seconds

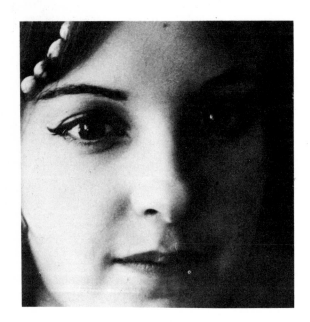

25 seconds

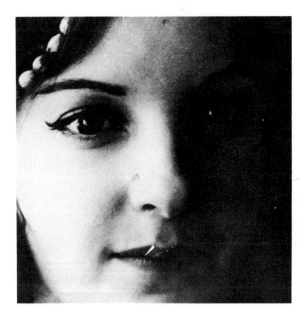

30 seconds

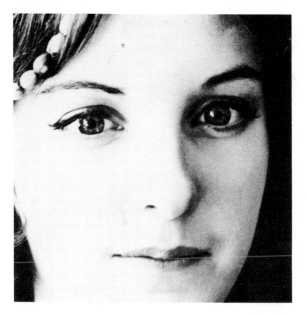

15 seconds

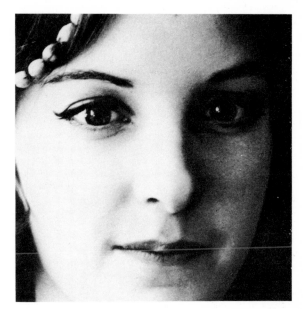

20 seconds

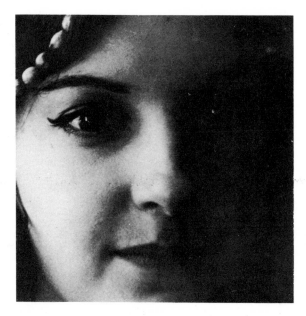

35 seconds

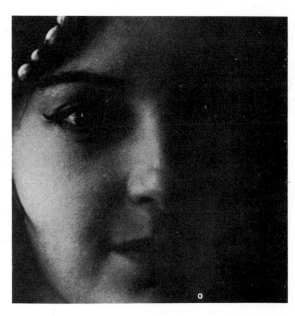

40 seconds

A series of test exposures made with three-inch pieces, or chips, of paper. You can use smaller chips, say two inches, but they won't give you as much reliable information. Chips as small as one inch are relatively useless.

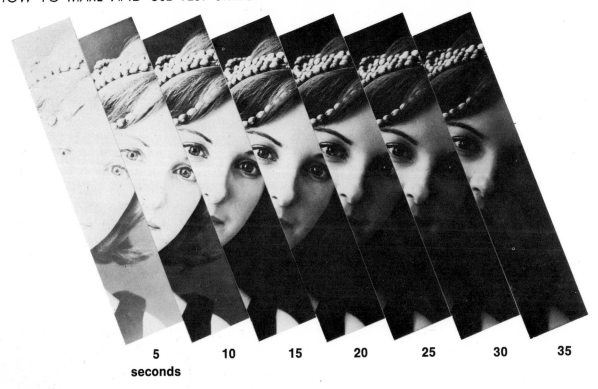

5 10 15 20 25 30 35
seconds

Duplicate-image test strips made by exposing all the pieces of paper to the same part of the image. They were positioned at an angle to give us a good sampling of all the important tone areas of the image. They give us the basic exposure and tell us what various parts of the image would look like if they were lightened (dodged) or darkened (burned-in). These strips tell us much more than a simple two-inch strip made with the 5–5–5–5 method.

● Duplicate-Image Test Strips

An ordinary test strip will usually work very well, but there are times when it won't. The problem is that each of the test exposures falls in a different part of the picture. Sometimes these areas are so unlike in their exposure requirements that the best exposure on the strip might be correct for only the area in which it falls. For example, a test strip shows that step three (fifteen seconds) has exactly the right exposure, yet a full-size print proves that this is too much exposure for all the rest of the picture.

We can easily get around this difficulty by using several strips of paper instead of just one. As usual, we position a strip by running it across all the picture areas for which we think we'll need specific exposure information. We give the first strip a five-second exposure. Then we start exposing other strips in exactly the same position, giving them respectively ten, fifteen, twenty, and

twenty-five seconds. We end up with five strips, each with a single exposure on it.

They should be developed simultaneously for a preselected optimum time. Though it is a little like playing with wet spaghetti, you should have no trouble. When you are through, you have five duplicate images, except that they vary in tone.

After the strips are fixed, lay them side by side on the back of a tray and examine them under the bright hypo light. You will probably see that none of them shows you the best exposure for the

62

entire picture but that, among them, they tell you all you need to know. One strip might show you that ten seconds would be right for the bottom of the picture, another that twenty seconds would do for the top. Others might indicate that a certain area needs twenty-five seconds and another area five seconds. This might seem like a ridiculous situation, but it is not. The problem can easily be handled by simple dodging and burning-in (pages 71ff.). These are things we do nearly all the time in ordinary printing.

The other types of test strips wouldn't give you all this information, or even come close to it. However, these duplicate-image strips consume more paper and take more time. Even so, they are both practical and economical in the long run because of the quality of exposure information they yield. Furthermore, they will give you accurate times for dodging and burning-in, which other types of exposure strips do not.

• Full-Sheet Exposure Tests

Every now and then you should make duplicate-image tests using full sheets of paper, rather than strips. You should do it only with pictures you really care about, of course. Otherwise, you would find it hard to justify the expense and time. The idea is that by carefully studying full-size tests, you can learn many things about the finer points of printing that you might ordinarily miss. It is unnecessary to tell you not to overdo it: your wallet tells you that. Nevertheless, you should overrule this prohibition once in a while—as a useful educational expense.

A good way to use full-sheet tests is to tape them up on the wall and study them for a few days. Vary the light intensity from time to time. Look at them close up, then from various other distances until you are across the room from them. These light and distance variations can teach you a lot.

• Honor Your Test Strips

You will soon see that making test strips is so easy that you could do it in your sleep. This could lead you to treat them with disrespect, which would be a very serious mistake. You should always remember that the most important step in becoming an expert printer is making handsome test strips that are properly exposed, processed, and cared for. Furthermore, good test strips can be your teachers, because there is very little that you need to know about printing that they can't teach you. Thus, if you are serious about your creative work you will learn to honor them.

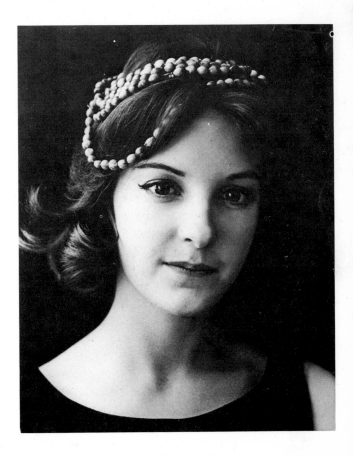

A straight print (not dodged, burned-in, or otherwise manipulated) made with a twenty-second exposure.

HOW TO MAKE AND USE A WORK PRINT

A work print is simply a preliminary study print that still needs to have work done on it in the form of cropping, dodging, burning-in, bleaching, or dye retouching. However, in terms of having the correct basic exposure and contrast it should be a high-quality picture. The idea is to have a printed image to study, for days or even weeks, before making a final commitment concerning how it will be treated in a finished print. Some people like to work this way; others don't. After you have tried it a few times, make your choice.

The purpose is to delay your decisions somewhat in order to give you a chance to see your pictures better. After you have made a few prints you will see why this is a useful idea. In our enthusiasm for seeing new pictures enlarged for the first time we often make mistakes, even to the point of producing prints of gruesome quality. At the time, however, we see them with eyes of love and utterly fail to see how awful they are. Later, we awaken, see the sorry fruits of our labors, and condemn ourselves as artistic incompetents. This is very hard on the morale, as any photographer can tell you.

The way around this morass is to be very tentative the first time you print a new roll of pictures. Instead of getting either tricky or hasty, slow yourself down and severely limit your objectives: (1) make a high-quality contact sheet and mark it up carefully, (2) make a high-quality test strip and analyze it in detail, and (3) make a high-quality basic print. This means a correctly exposed print, of the right contrast, that hasn't been dodged, burned-in, bleached, or otherwise manipulated.

By thus limiting your objectives, you greatly lessen your chances of failure. Since a work print is only a tentative way of looking ahead to what the final print will be, how can it really be wrong at this point? Indeed, some people carry this idea so far that they are quite satisfied with really sloppy work prints, finding that they can use them quite well in making decisions concerning final prints. Because these poor prints are both tentative and useful, they could hardly be considered failures.

Some people make cruddy work prints because they are lazy or can't do any better. On the other hand, skilled photographers sometimes do it when they are in a terrible hurry. With their quality standards lowered they can bang out prints almost as fast as they can move. Because of their long experience they can easily tell how a poor-quality work print will translate into a high-quality finished one.

As a beginner you are totally incapable of this, and please don't forget it. Though it will take you extra work and time, you should always make the best work prints that you possibly can. Otherwise, your sensitivity to print quality will not develop properly and you won't learn the difference between good prints and bad ones. For you a tacky work print is about as useful as a broken neck. See?

• No Cropping

It is not advisable to crop work prints, because you might crop out things that you would leave in if you had more chance to consider them. Unfortunately, many enlarger negative carriers cut off some of the image, sometimes enough to ruin certain pictures. Therefore, advanced photographers and professionals usually file out their carriers enough to permit all of the frame and some of the border to print, which gives them work prints with neat black edges. Filing out just the right amount is fairly important. When the negative is in position there should be about one sixteenth inch of border showing all the way around.

• Size of Work Print

It is easiest to assess the possibilities of a work print if you make it the same size that your finished print will be. After you have had some experience in printing, however, you will find that half size is entirely adequate—and more economical, of course. You may even want to work quarter size.

Some people go to custom labs, where they have enlargers that will project a whole roll at a time to make "enlarged contact sheets," usually 11×14 or 16×20. Though they look exactly like 8×10 contacts the images are considerably larger and easier to see. This is certainly the easiest way to get work prints, but it is more expensive than making them yourself.

• Things You Need

Though most of this list was given earlier, it seems about time to repeat it for your convenience. There are a few additions and omissions, however.

Negatives to print
Contacts
Enlarger
Enlarging easel
A no. 4 sable brush
Silicone anti-static cloth
Focusing magnifier (optional)
Focusing paper
Timer, metronome, or watch
Double-weight enlarging paper, regular or resin-coated (RC)
Printing filters (optional: for variable-contrast paper)
Scissors or paper cutter
Pencil
Note pad
Safelight(s)
Thermometer
Towel(s)
Dektol print developer
Kodak Indicator Stop Bath
First hypo
Second hypo
A hypo light
Print-inspection board
An 11×14 piece of cardboard
Tracing paper (optional)
Mount boards
Perma Wash (unless you are using RC paper)
Funnel
Chemical-storage bottles
Photographic blotters (optional)
Masking tape
A china marker

Most of these items have already been explained, but some have not.

Focusing magnifier: An optical device that you put on the focusing paper directly under the enlarger lens, to help you see when you have the negative in critically sharp focus. The useful kind is called a "high-magnification grain focuser." Other types are either useless or aggravating. If your close-up vision is not so good you will need such a magnifier, otherwise not.

Focusing paper: A sheet of printing paper that you put in the easel for focusing and cropping your pictures. Since it is of the same thickness as the paper you print on, you may be sure that the print will be in as sharp focus as the focusing paper. If you have an easel with adjustable masking blades it is convenient to draw dark-pencil frame lines on the paper, four in all, at distances of ½, 1, 1½, and 2 inches from the edge. They make setting the masking blades easy and fast.

Scissors or paper cutter: Though it is very convenient to have a paper-trimming board in the darkroom you can get along for years without one. If you use scissors to cut printing paper into halves, quarters, or strips, make yourself some little cardboard templates—5×7, 4×8, 4×5, and 1×8. For accurate trimming, put a template on the back of a sheet of printing paper, using it as a ruler for drawing a line. Even under a safelight you can see well enough to accurately cut along this line with scissors.

Pencil: When you are making test strips and work prints it is a good idea to write notes on the back of them concerning the aperture settings, exposure times, paper contrast grades, and so on. Otherwise, you may soon forget the information or get it confused. With regular paper use ordinary pencil, but *do not use* a ball-point pen or felt-tip markers. With resin-coated (RC) paper use a china marker, but write lightly with it.

Note pad: For more extensive notes, use a note pad. When you make work prints it is with the intention of duplicating them later, except for additional manipulation such as dodging and burning-in. Having good notes will make this fast and easy.

Print-inspection board: to lay prints or test strips on for examination under the hypo light. Can also be used for bleaching prints. The back of a tray will work fine, but a panel of plastic or glass is better. If you use glass, cover one side with black Con-Tact paper, the other with white. It is helpful to view prints against these colors; and the paper shatterproofs the glass.

Masking tape: In photography, masking tape

comes close to being the universal tool, so you should always have some near at hand.

• Step by Step to Make a Work Print

If you have made some test strips you already know how to make enlargements, because test strips *are* enlargements. However, to pull things together and make the work easier we will use this step by step schedule for making prints.

1. Assemble all the items on the list and set up the chemical processing trays.

2. Organize the negatives, contacts, printing paper, scissors, anti-static cloth, etc., on the dry side of your darkroom.

3. Select a contact sheet and examine it to refresh your mind concerning which negative you had already decided to print first.

4. Find the negative in its glassine envelope.

5. Clean it carefully, then check the effectiveness of the cleaning job, picking off remaining dust with a brush.

6. Put the negative in the enlarger.

7. Open the lens all the way.

8. Turn on the safelight(s) and turn off the white light.

9. Turn on the enlarger light.

10. Position the enlarger head and easel to give you the largest possible full-frame image on the focusing paper.

11. Focus the image sharply.

12. Turn off the enlarger light.

13. Cut a full sheet of 8×10 paper into 1×8-inch strips, returning all but one to the package.

14. Stop down the enlarger lens two or three stops.

15. Expose and process a test strip.

16. Examine the test strip under the hypo light to decide which is the best exposure on it for the work print. If the best exposure would fall between two areas, average their exposure times.

17. Set the timer for the time decided upon.

18. Change the aperture setting if necessary.

19. Put printing paper in the easel and make an exposure.

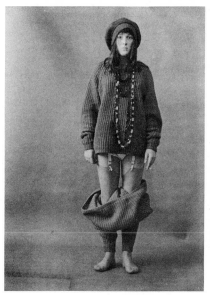

A

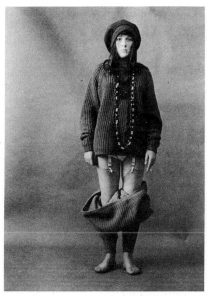

B

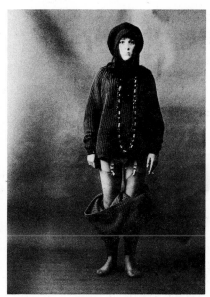

C

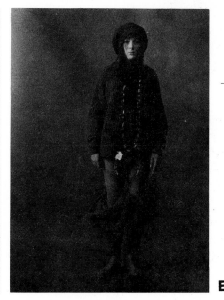

D

E

20. Make pencil notes on the back of it and on your note pad.

21. Process, wash, and dry the work print.

In order to make it complete, the list was made a little long, but don't let that bother you. Instead of throwing up your hands in despair, read through it line by line. You will then agree that any six-year-old could follow it.

A good work print should be properly exposed and made on paper of the right contrast grade. With one exception, B, these prints are either badly exposed or of the wrong contrast. A is properly exposed but two contrast grades too flat. C, also properly exposed, is two grades too contrasty. D and E are on the correct paper, but D is a stop underexposed, while E is one stop (100 per cent) overexposed.

● Work Print – Finished Print

With many a picture, you will find that a well-made work print is as far as you need to go. In such case a work print and a finished one are the same thing, a finished print merely being one that needs nothing more done to it. This is one reason you were asked to work carefully: instead of settling for a foul-ball work print you may find that you've hit a home run.

Work prints are usually called "straight prints," incidentally, but you can call them whatever you like. It is good to keep track of the twists and turns of photographic jargon, yet we are only talking here about prints that haven't been fussed with. They've been correctly exposed on the right-contrast paper, then correctly processed. That's all—no manipulation.

There are some who claim that there is no such thing as a work, or straight, print that can't be improved with a little dodging, burning-in, or bleaching. Thus it would be incorrect to say that a work print could also be a finished print at the same time. Though this view is a little precious, it happens to be a very useful one for people who are just learning the craft of photography. It would therefore be wise for you to adopt it for the time being. Assume that a work print can always be improved, no matter how good it already looks. Following this concept has turned many a person into a master printer.

A little more concerning the jargon: The terms work print, basic print, study print, first print, straight print, fast print, and trial print are synonymous. So are finished print, final print, fully realized print, and manipulated print. There is nothing precious about any of these terms, though people tend to use them as if there were. Be satisfied if they merely help you keep track of what you are reading.

● Cropping L's

When you set out to study a work print it is convenient to start with the cropping. If you trim one or more sides it may look better. Cropping means trimming, that's all. You can sail right into the cropping problem with a paper cutter or scissors if you like, but what if you make a mistake? What if you change your mind about how it should be cropped? Then you end up with a mutilated and useless work print. It is better not to cut it up at all. However, this still leaves you with the problem of visualizing what different croppings would look like, which is rather difficult for beginners.

The simple answer is to make yourself some visual-aid equipment in the form of "cropping L's," which are merely L shapes cut out of cardboard or paper. By laying them on a print and moving them around, you can get them to enclose a rectangle of any dimensions you like. That is, you can see what any cropping would look like without having to cut up your print.

When you find the cropping you like best you can draw it right on the print, if you like. Just use your cropping L's as rulers and draw lines with a china marker. For the sake of neatness you might sharpen the marker somewhat with a used razor

Cardboard cropping L's are used to tell what a picture will look like when its area is cut down (cropped) in various ways.

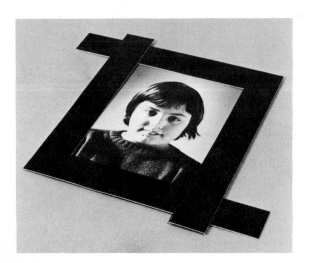

blade. If you later change your mind about the cropping, wipe it off with cotton soaked in lighter fluid.

Cut out your cropping L's neatly, or their ragged or crooked edges will throw your aesthetic judgement out of kilter. We already have enough trouble with this in photography without having to ask for it. You can make the best cropping L's from a photographic mount board that has both a white and a black side. Depending on the tone of the print, you will prefer one color or the other, but sometimes you will wish to try both. A wallboard knife and ruler are good for cutting mount board, provided you make four or five strokes for each cut. If you try to do it in one stroke the knife will go everywhere except where you want it to.

You will find that fourteen-inch cropping L's two inches wide are about right for 8×10 prints. Some people also like to have small ones to carry around with them, so they can practice cropping snapshots and pictures in magazines. It's fun.

• Use a Note Board

One makes a work print in order to have something tangible to think about while deciding how the final print should be made. It is rather like thinking up original things to think about—not so easy when you try it. One must look at the work print inch by inch, notice every single thing in it, try to decide what it does for the picture as a whole, ponder about whether it has the right tone, try to visualize what it would look like if its tone were changed, and so on. This requires genuine original thought, which we have to force ourselves into—the ego being naturally lazy. Or we can trick ourselves into it.

One of the ways of conning yourself into doing heavy-duty mental and perceptual work is to intentionally make a real production of it. An easy enough way to do this is to tape your print to the clean back of a mount board, centering it well and taking care to do a neat job of it. This gives

the work print considerable importance and prestige. The idea now is to ponder it from time to time (it's best not to do it all at once), trying to decide what you should do in making the finished print. Record your decisions neatly in pencil on the mount board around the print, judiciously making little diagrams, arrows, and asterisks, too. Take pains to make your work look important, and you will soon find yourself believing that it is. When you do come to believe, your work will be half done, even if you have to change some of your decisions later.

Except for neat cropping lines, don't write or diagram anything on the print itself, because your markings would change the visuals of your picture so radically that you wouldn't be able to make well-balanced decisions with respect to it. In effect, you would be analyzing one picture while attempting to make decisions concerning a different one.

Though you will be considering doing dodging, burning-in, bleaching, and dye retouching, they all boil down to just one thing: making certain tones either lighter or darker. The thing you must try to visualize is what difference it would make. However, until you've had quite a bit of experience in printing, you will have no substantial basis for knowing, one way or the other.

Thus you are forced to either psych out your pictures (follow your strongest whims or rely on your innate visual sensitivity) or do things arbitrarily just to see what happens. Fortunately, both approaches are quite good enough. Whatever you do, you'll make mistakes anyway, but they should be considered as textbooks from which you can learn. In a sense, the entire art of photography is founded on mistakes—so don't get uptight about them.

It would help if you were to try to see your decisions as important while you are making them and your mistakes as of no importance whatever. It is a matter of learning to cleverly con yourself.

An approach that is a little fancier may suit your legitimate need to convince yourself of the importance of thoroughly studying a work print even when you don't yet know what you are really looking for. Put a clean piece of tracing paper over the print, neatly taping it to the edge of the mount board. Now you can make impressive little diagrams right over the print without harming it any. Then when you want to see what it actually looks like again you merely lift up the tracing paper. And if you don't like your drawings you can start over again with a fresh piece of paper. Another alternative is to use a sheet of clear plastic, drawing on it with a china marker, and removing mistakes with cotton soaked in lighter fluid. It's re-usable, too.

Since you don't yet really know anything about printing, you shouldn't expect your notes and

lines to embody the wisdom of Solomon. He didn't know anything about photography, anyway. But you should at least *do* the work, because it is a good habit to get into and will make it easier for you to force yourself to see better. Absurd as it may sound, all artists have to force themselves to learn to see, it is such hard work. Whoever says otherwise is telling you a fairy tale.

A work print taped to the back of a used mount board, then taped to a door, where it can be studied at leisure. As you study a work print you can make notes to yourself on the edges of the board. This will help you make up your mind with respect to what you should do when you make your final print; that is, where you should crop, dodge, burn-in, bleach, etc.

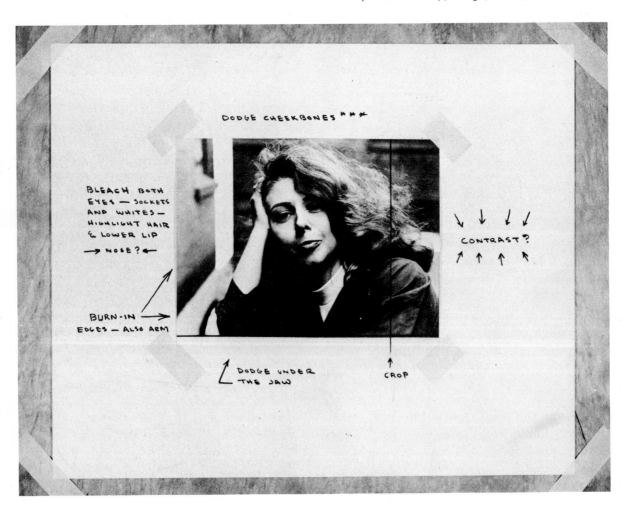

HOW AND WHEN TO DODGE AND BURN-IN

Dodging is a simple technique for lightening areas of a print, burning-in a technique for darkening them. Though this doesn't sound like much, it is the most subtle and exciting part of printing. In only an hour or so you can learn the basic skills and immediately begin using them effectively on pictures in which local tonal adjustments are obviously necessary, yet you can spend a lifetime learning their nuances. Thus we could say that both techniques are extremely easy but endlessly sophisticated, too. The results that you can get with them will keep you fascinated with printing for many years.

● Things You Need

Since you will be making enlargements again, you can use the list given in the previous chapter. However, we will add a few items that are used in making tools for dodging and burning-in.

Scissors
Pencil
A 10-inch piece of straight coat-hanger wire
Masking tape
Two round cardboard disks ¾ inch and 2 inches in diameter
Three sheets of 11×14-inch light cardboard

● Making Your Tools

To make a dodging tool, or dodger, tape the two cardboard disks to opposite ends of the wire. Though you can easily make additional dodgers using cardboard in other sizes and shapes, you will very seldom need to. If you do, the easiest thing is to temporarily tape the new shapes onto the old ones, so you won't have to go looking around for more wire.

You will need three burning-in tools made of cardboard about 11×14 inches, two with single round holes in the middle of them, one without a hole. The holes should be about three quarters of an inch and two inches in diameter. Since you will probably be looking at these cardboards for years to come, you might as well cut the holes neatly.

Though these tools are very simple, as you see, they are like clay in the hands of a master potter: amazing things can be done with them.

● How to Dodge a Print

You dodge an area in a print by temporarily blocking off the light that is falling upon it from the enlarger. You can do this by simply sticking your hand under the lens for a moment, so that a shadow is cast on the area. Indeed, many printers do most of their dodging with one or both of their hands. However, beginners should stick to dodgers, because they are easier to use with precision.

Your dodger is simply a shadow caster, and with the two disks you can get any size shadow you want by merely varying their distance from the lens. With the larger one you can even block off the light altogether, if you wish.

When you cast a shadow on an area for part of the exposure time, you lighten it in the resulting print. If you dodge it for the entire time it will come out white. By varying the proportion of

Drawing of a dodging tool in use. It casts a shadow, which should be moved around during the dodging period so that the dodged area will blend with the part of the image surrounding it. Note that the wire handle of the dodger also casts a shadow that must be blended in.

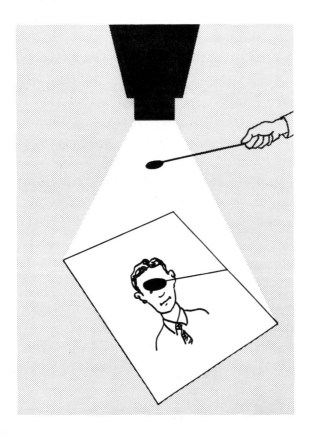

dodging time to exposure time you can lighten it to any degree you wish. However, it is usually not good to dodge a given area for more than 50 per cent of the total exposure time. If you do, it will generally come out looking flat, washed out, or muddy. If your negative is too thin, even that percentage is too high. Remember that a thin negative is one that has been underexposed and/or underdeveloped.

If you hold the dodger still while you are using it, it will make a round silhouette of itself on your picture. Occasionally this is a good idea, but usually not. Ordinarily, we want our pictures to show no evidence whatever of having been manipulated in any way, so we have to subtly blend the dodged area in with the rest of the picture. We do this by simply moving the dodger around constantly while we are using it. Easy as pie.

Perhaps the hardest thing is to learn to keep track of the dodging time while we are dodging. It is a little like the old patting-your-head-and-rubbing-your-stomach trick. The best thing is to make some dry runs, practicing until you've gotten the time problem sorted out. The easiest way is to let a photographic timer take care of the basic exposure time, while under your breath you count out seconds for dodging. Using a metronome requires a little more mental agility, a watch or clock still more. However, thousands of people time their dodging this way, so you see that it is actually possible.

You may sometimes have a problem with the shadow cast by the wire part of the dodger, because it can make light streaks on prints. The easy solution is to keep varying the angle at which this shadow crosses the image, for then it will leave no evidence of itself. Thus you must move the disk around in one pattern, the shadow of the wire in another. After a little practice you will find it easy.

● How to Burn-In a Print

To burn-in an area, you give it some extra exposure after the basic exposure time is up, at the same time blocking off this extra light from the rest of the picture, which doesn't need it. One does this with a burning-in tool, the hole letting light through, the cardboard shielding areas that already have enough exposure. For blending purposes we constantly move the cardboard around during the additional exposure.

When the enlarger light is on, the image shows up on the cardboard, its sharpness depending on the distance between the cardboard and the lens. When the board is nearly touching the printing paper the picture is so sharply defined that one can see exactly where the hole is letting light through to darken an area. In order to take advantage of this you should use a burning-in tool quite a bit larger than your printing paper, an 11×14-inch board being about the right size for an 8×10 print.

You usually don't need this precision, however, because areas that need to be darkened are generally defined rather vaguely. With the cardboard held much closer to the lens you can still see the image well enough to see what you are doing, even if it is very fuzzy. Varying this distance also permits you to control the size of the area that is being burned-in at a given moment, aided by the fact that you have holes of two sizes to work with. Using the small hole close to the printing paper, it is possible to burn-in a large area by moving it back and forth like a paintbrush or a spray gun, but this would be unduly laborious. Starting out with the right-size circle of light on the printing paper would be better. However, the paintbrush approach is good for darkening areas that are long and very narrow.

Dodging time is usually limited to about 50 per cent of the basic exposure, and there are just so many areas that can be dodged in the time available. In burning-in we don't have these limitations. You can burn-in as many areas as you like, each one for as long as you like. It is not uncommon to see a person use five to ten minutes' worth of burning-in on a single print. Frequently, individual areas are so "blocked up" that they need two to three minutes before they get any tone in them.

This means that some parts of a negative may be so heavily exposed (and dark) that light can hardly get through them at all. overshot

It is nice to know that you can make selected parts of your prints as dark as you please, but such long burning-in times get very tedious. However, you can shorten them very considerably by opening up the enlarger lens all the way after you have given the basic exposure. There are two other problems with such long times: one is that you may heat up your enlarger too much and damage it and your negative; the answer here is to burn-in a while, let it cool off, then burn-in

Drawing of a burning-in card in use. This is a way of selectively darkening parts of the image after it has been given the basic exposure. For blending purposes the card is moved around constantly during the burning-in period. Otherwise it would create an obvious round spot with sharp edges.

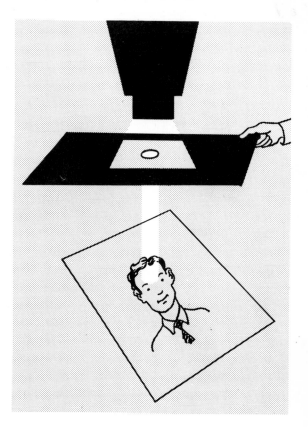

some more, etc. The other is that your negative may "pop," like a color slide popping out of focus in a slide projector. This would throw the image far out of focus and ruin the print.

There is a good answer for this, though a little time-consuming: make your print all the way through with a "prepopped" negative. Do it this way: turn on the enlarger light until the negative pops (warps), then focus the image on the focusing paper. Turn off the light and immediately put printing paper in the easel and make the basic exposure—while the negative is still popped and in focus. Then immediately do whatever burning-in you wish to do.

You use the cardboard with no hole in it to burn-in the corners and edges of pictures. You let the light shine on one edge or corner of the printing paper at a time, making a blend by constantly moving the cardboard back and forth. However, you can use a dodger instead of a cardboard and burn-in all the edges and corners at the same time. You can do this by holding the larger disk right under the lens and moving it constantly up and down between the lens and the paper.

• When to Do It

Subtly changing the tones of local areas is absurdly easy with the techniques you have just read about. The problem is in deciding which areas need changing and how far the changes should go. You do this mainly by "feel." That is, you observe and respond to your emotional reactions to pictures. You let them guide you. For example, if an area is too light you may feel it as being washed out, weak, insubstantial, unreal, or lacking in surface detail and solidity. The area simply bothers you, though you may not be able to put your feelings into words. Similarly, you may feel a too-dark area is heavy, morbid, dirty, unreal, or unduly obscure. In either case, you wish to manipulate the tone of the areas enough to change your feelings about them from negative to positive. You merely want them to look and feel right.

People usually have little trouble deciding whether they want things lighter, darker, or left alone. Most of the time, they almost automatically know whether they want to dodge or burn-in. With a little experience they learn how far they wish to go in either direction. For most of their pictures they don't need the help of a teacher. However, there are many little tricks in printing that people don't usually learn unless they are told about them. We will now look into some of them.

• Faces and Skin (Flesh) Tone

There are many things in pictures that can be too light or too dark without our minding it at all—trees, bushes, and rocks, for example. However, when it comes to such things as faces and skin tone we mind a lot. Consequently, they probably have more tone manipulation done on them than any other subject in photography, most of it done by dodging.

We will start with faces that are about two inches or longer. Usually we can dodge them with the two-inch disk, so that the skin and all the features get lightened at once. Sometimes this takes too much of the brilliance out of the eyes, however, so they must be left undodged. The solution is to use the smaller disk, moving it around above the face for the *entire* exposure, or most of it. For a two-to-three-inch face it should nearly be touching the printing paper.

A portrait may need only highlight dodging, which is very good for making skin look more alive. Just lighten the highlights that are already there, using the small dodger again. If you try to make them where none exist the dodging will look phony and the face distorted. Usually you can restrict yourself to the cheekbones, jaw line and the top two thirds of the forehead, because the large highlights usually fall in these areas.

If the eyes are sunken in shadow or have dark bags under them you may have to dodge them, even if they lose some of their brilliance. You have to make a compromise here.

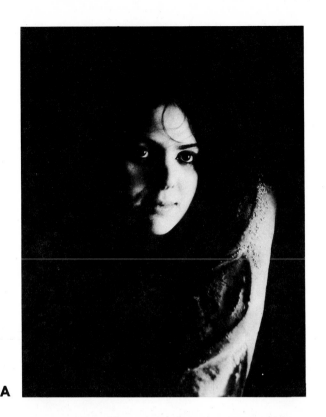

A

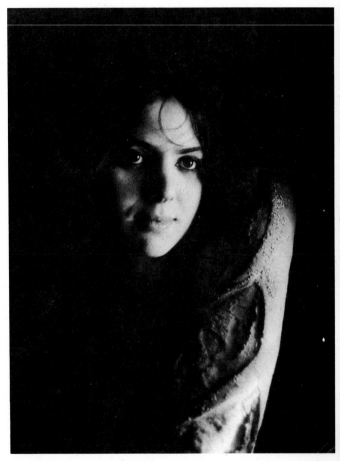

C

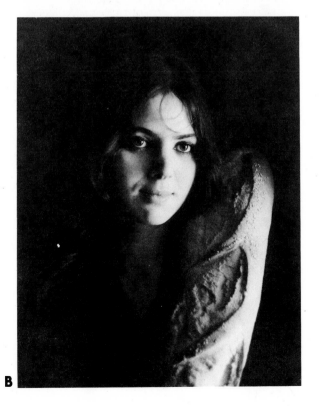

B

A is a straight print made on a no. 5 paper, which makes the face a bit too strong and harsh. Print B, on a no. 2 paper, makes the face soft enough, but the rest of the print is too gray. Print C, also on a no. 2, has the same basic exposure as B, but the edges have been heavily burned-in to make them darker.

Quite often the two sides of a face are much too far apart in tone. In this case, expose for the highlight side and dodge for the dark side. Thus the light side will take care of itself, while the other side is being lightened with the dodger. If you dodge as much as you can without making the dark side look muddy and the tonal difference between the two sides is still too great, your only other alternative is to use a lower-contrast paper. You may still need to dodge, however.

For a face smaller than an inch you will have to use the small dodger, which will dodge it all at once and wash out the eyes somewhat. However, you probably won't mind this with a face so small.

We don't use burning-in much on faces, because it is a little harder to control. It is mainly used for light-struck, washed-out ears and patches of hair. However, it is fairly easy to burn-in a whole or half face. The problem is with light-struck cheekbones and noses, for it is hard to get the burned-in tones to blend. If an ear or hair doesn't blend exactly we don't mind so much.

● **Skies**

People generally like to burn-in the skies in their landscape pictures. It makes clear skies look richer and deeper, clouded ones more dramatic with the clouds more clearly defined. With clear skies it is generally good to burn-in for a tonal gradation ranging from nearly white at the horizon to a medium gray at the top of the picture. If a sky prints too dark near the horizon you can dodge it with the shadow of a pencil during the basic exposure. Because skies are seldom lighted evenly you will probably have to burn-in one side more than the other.

Burning-in for a smooth tonal gradation is very easy. Using the cardboard without a hole, start burning-in at the top of the picture while moving the card down toward the horizon. The instant it gets there, start it back up again. Keep repeating this until the time is up. Simple enough.

You may or may not want a graded tone for a cloudy sky; it depends on what the clouds look like. And you may wish to combine dodging with burning-in. For example, you might dodge a cloud entirely for the whole basic exposure, which would leave it a blank white if the print were developed at that point. Instead of developing, however, you could burn-in the whole sky, including the cloud. Thus the cloud would come out with its normal tone, whereas the sky around it would be darkened considerably. This would make the cloud much more dramatic. We were speaking of a cloud that was lighter than the sky to begin with, of course. Starting with a darker cloud, we could burn it in after dodging the sky, which would also be dramatic.

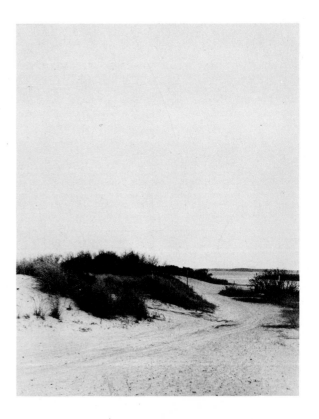

A straight print (above) of this sand dune makes a rather uninteresting picture. However, extensive burning-in brought out dramatic clouds in the sky (print at right). The lower corners of the picture were also burned-in and the center of the dune dodged somewhat.

76

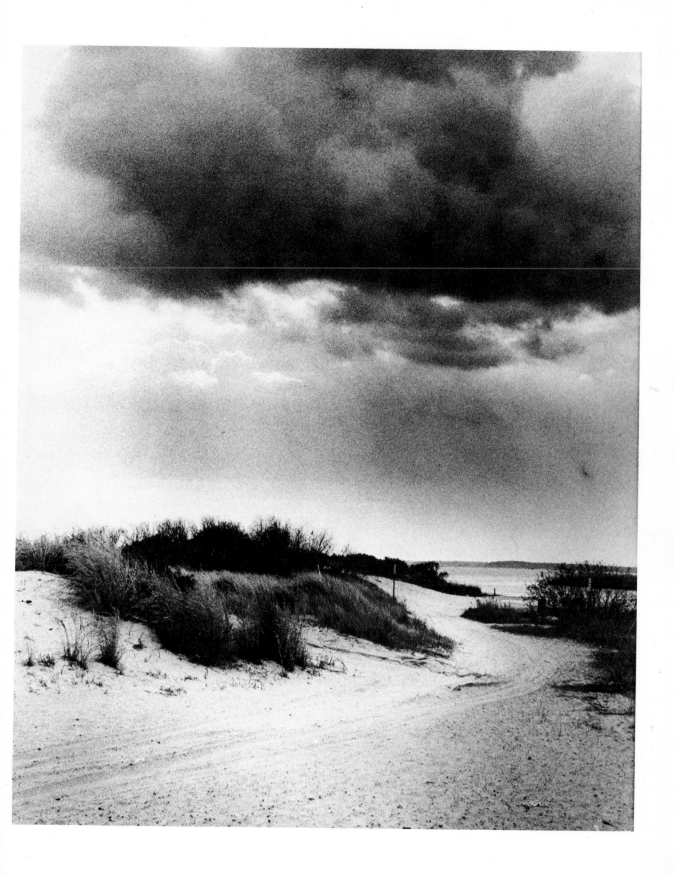

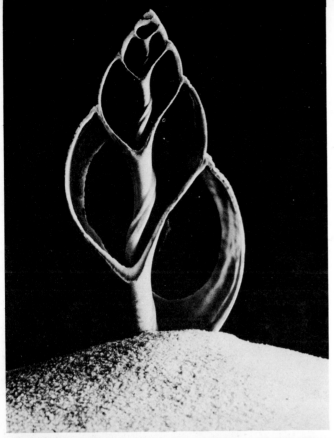

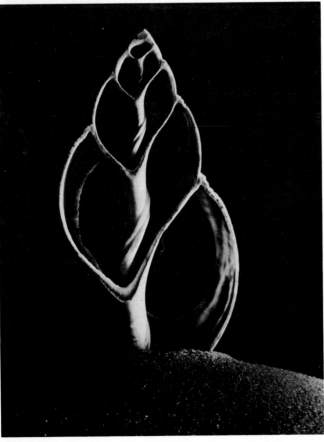

Clouds are fun to mess with, because you can make such gross mistakes without anyone being able to tell. This is a far cry from portraiture, in which your dodging and burning-in mistakes stand out like castor oil in a lemon pie.

● Corners

Some photographers like to burn-in the corners of all their pictures, but usually not very much. They sometimes call it "strengthening the corners." Burning-in strengthens corners by simply darkening them, which gives them more substance and weight (in the visual arts, tone is often equated with weight).

Darkened corners also confirm and emphasize the rectangular shape of the image, which in many pictures is a little ambiguous due to undetected optical illusions. These illusions seem to warp the pictures somewhat. However, trying to make it obvious that a picture is exactly rectangular must seem like a strange preoccupation, because rectangles per se are so totally uninteresting. Well, this is precisely why we use rectangular shapes for pictures and frames. They are such a bore that they don't distract from the pictures themselves. However, if a picture doesn't seem to be exactly rectangular our attention is attracted to its proportions rather than to the picture itself—so we remedy this distraction by burning-in the corners.

Another reason for burning-in corners is to lead the viewer's attention to the center of the picture and hold it there. We get a kind of tunnel or bull's-eye effect, in which he feels almost compelled to look where we wish him to, instead of letting his eyes wander elsewhere.

Finally, we burn-in corners to subordinate things in the picture that are too close to them.

In print above the bright foreground attracts too much attention from the shell. In print below it has been heavily burned-in to make it less conspicuous.

One usually organizes a picture so that important things are somewhere near the middle and things of less importance near the edges or corners, which ordinarily guarantees that the latter won't be unduly noticed. However, strong "centers of interest" are created if things get *too* close to edges or corners. A center of interest is merely something that attracts the eye. Now, it happens that things in corners can create by far the most powerful centers.

When we burn-in things we usually lessen their visibility somewhat, because we reduce the contrast and darken the tone. Thus we have an easy way to defuse unwanted centers of interest. It sometimes doesn't work, however, because in some pictures burning-in will emphasize something rather than de-emphasize it. Then we have to resort to a special technique called "flashing." Though it is not quite the same as burning-in it is done in almost the same way. It will effectively subordinate areas near the picture corners.

You do flashing with "raw light" from the enlarger. After making the basic exposure you remove the negative, stop down the lens all the way, and burn-in the corners in the usual way. Make a record of the burning-in time, because you can use it again for other pictures.

● The Bottoms of Pictures

The bottoms of pictures frequently need burning-in, especially if they are areas of flooring, sidewalk, or roadway. When bottoms are too light they weaken pictures, make them seem insecurely balanced, and attract the eyes to the wrong places. Usually it is good to have the lighter weights (tones) near the tops of pictures, the heavier ones near their bottoms. Burning-in and dodging help us distribute weight.

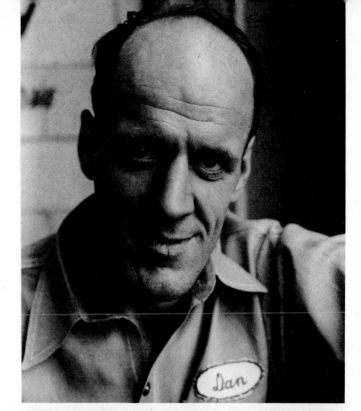

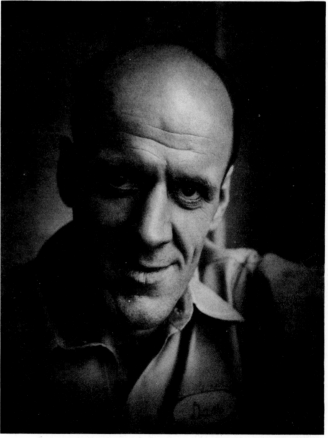

In a straight print (top) the background is a little distracting. It was toned down by flashing (below), which is simply burning-in done without a negative being in the enlarger negative carrier.

79

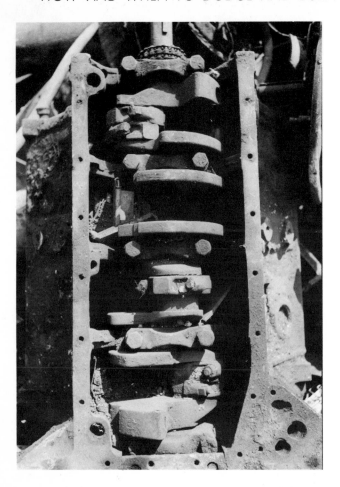
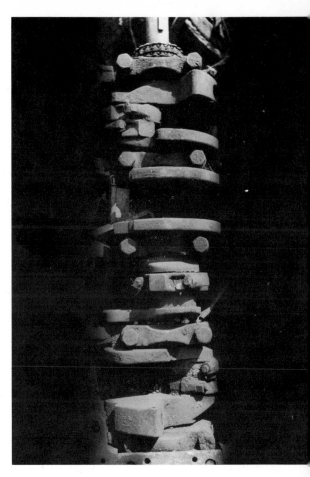

A straight print of a piece of old junk (left) makes a picture that is a bit too complicated and messy. Heavy flashing (right) simplifies and dramatizes the image.

• Heavy Shadows

Sometimes shadows get so dark that it is hard to see into them, and parts of the picture are lost in darkness. Such shadows are said to be "closed" or "blocked up." If there is good detail in the shadow areas of the negative they can be opened up (lightened) by dodging, but if they are relatively empty (clear) we can only dodge a little bit —or we'll get mud or pea soup.

• Unwanted Things

In some pictures there are things we would like to get rid of altogether. If we can't get rid of them by cropping we may be able to use dodging or burning-in; it depends mainly on the tonal areas that surround them. By heavily burning-in things in black areas we can lose them in darkness. By heavily dodging things in white areas we can lose them in lightness. Since the things we wish to eliminate may not be surrounded by either black or white we may not be able to completely obliterate them this way. However, we can lessen their visibility somewhat by making them more like their surroundings in tone. Things that are alike get lost in each other.

Separation

We have just seen that when things blend together they get lost in each other, which is sometimes a good thing, because it lessens their power to distract the eye. The important things in pictures should have "good separation," however. This means that there should be good tonal contrast between them, so that you can easily tell where one leaves off and the other begins. They will also have high visibility, which is what we usually want for the most important things in our pictures. What can they accomplish if people can't see them?

To separate things, we simply make them tonally unlike—by dodging, burning-in, or both. For example, if a house in a picture blends too much with the sky, we can make one of them lighter by dodging, or one of them darker by burning-in. Or we can make one lighter and the other darker.

Local Contrast

Earlier, we saw that graded-contrast papers and printing filters are used to give us the correct over-all contrast for a given picture. However, we often have pictures that are contrasty in some areas and flat in others, so that a single paper grade or filter cannot solve the over-all contrast problem. For example, we might have a picture calling for no. 1 contrast on the left and no. 4 on the right. This sometimes happens when we get "lens flare" from direct light striking the camera lens or from posing a subject in front of an area much brighter than itself.

The simple left-to-right problem can often be handled by "contrast dodging," in which one uses a variable-contrast paper and printing filters. You use two basic exposures, each of them given by dodging, and use a different filter for each exposure. To solve the above problem, for example,

you would use a no. 1 filter while exposing the left side of the picture and simultaneously shielding the other side from exposure by dodging. Then you would use a no. 4 filter to expose the right side while dodging the left.

To get a good blend you would move the dodging card back and forth from left to right for both exposures, just as in any other kind of dodging. Though it is an easy technique, one usually has to make a test strip for each filter, then make three or four final prints in order to get the blending just right.

Contrast dodging is a good technique, but there are few occasions for using it. One more frequently runs into local contrast problems that can be handled by ordinary dodging or burning-in on graded (single-contrast) paper. For example, try to imagine a picture of a family back yard. On one side of this picture is a sizable playhouse standing in front of a tall hedge. The contrast of the print is exactly right, except for the area around the playhouse, which is very flat. To correct for this flatness we merely dodge the house a bit (lighten it) and burn-in (darken) the shrubbery closest to it, thus building up the contrast between them.

Notice that we worked on only two things: the playhouse and the hedge. The rest of the flat side of the print wasn't touched. The point is that you can almost always liven up a whole area by selecting only a few things within it to work on. Furthermore, if you work on too many things you will nearly always give yourself away, because your dodging and burning-in will stand out like sore thumbs.

We can also *calm down* areas of a print by locally *reducing* contrast. For example, we might have another print of the same back yard in which the area around the playhouse is too contrasty instead of too flat. This could happen if it were photographed at a different time of day. In this case we would merely reverse our procedures. We would burn-in (darken) the house and dodge (lighten) the hedge, thus *reducing* the contrast between them. This would have the effect of reducing the contrast in that entire area, thus calming it down. If you have had difficulty in visualizing the material in the previous paragraphs, draw a little picture to help you. Since this is good for you, I have intentionally not provided an illustration.

• Space and Volume

Photography is a three-dimensional medium—some of the time. Any photograph whatever has two real dimensions, length and breadth, and the possibility of an illusional third dimension, depth. Though depth is only an illusion, we work with it all the time, like a sculptor manipulating his volumes. Illusions have their reality, too, for they are there and we can see them. We can also create, destroy, or otherwise manipulate them. Such being the reality of depth in a photograph, it makes good sense to call photography a three-dimensional medium.

Now, dodging and burning-in are two of the chief tools for depth manipulation in prints. We could say they are merely extensions of light, or lighting, which is the master tool. When we lighten or darken things in prints we are modifying the record of the effect that light was having upon them when they were photographed. Actually, we are falsifying the lighting data recorded in negatives, often to make prints look more real, more three-dimensional. In a sense, in order to tell the truth about things we have to use falsehoods. This is because we are working with illusions.

Photographs vary considerably in the amount of depth they have. When we look at some of them it is like looking through deep windows into space. We can "get into them," as they say, mentally participate in them as events taking place in space. We call them "open" prints.

However, most prints are "closed." They confront us with only surface, no depth, so that no amount of imagination will permit us to get into them. One characteristic of closed prints is that they are also "tight." The things in tight prints look so firmly glued into place that it is hard to imagine anything moving around or through them. Even air couldn't do it, because they have no "feeling of air space." Though the terms we are now using are intangible, stick with them, for they are an important part of the language of the visual arts. By making pictures you will come to understand them.

The first thing to do with a closed print is to open it up, which will immediately add depth to it. There is one technique so simple that even your dog could master it. It consists in using "arbitrary dodging," which simply means that you can be entirely arbitrary in choosing things to dodge, or even pay no attention to what you are dodging while you are doing it. Just wave the dodger around during the basic exposure. You can do roughly the same thing with "arbitrary burning-in," and of course you can do both. In the finished print there will be no evidence of either, except that it will be more loose, more open. These simple techniques break up the overtight structural integrity of the image, so that "the air can get between the bricks." Or we could say that they knock out some of the glue.

However, the effect may be too subtle for you to see it clearly. A sure way to guarantee a more tangible success is to be not quite so arbitrary. Follow this rule: lighten the lights and darken the darks. That is, pick out a few light areas and dodge them to make them even lighter, then pick some dark areas and burn them darker. With this formula we not only open up a print but strongly increase its three-dimensional quality. However, the lights and darks can still be selected almost arbitrarily. An important part of this trick is to not work on a total of too many areas. Just pick a few here and there. There is a related rule that you might also try: lighten the tops of things and darken their bottoms.

These techniques are often needed on prints

that seem to need nothing whatever done to them in the way of dodging or burning-in. A print may be technically excellent and still be as tight as a whale full of peanut butter. In this case, technical excellence would be equivalent to aesthetic mediocrity, so loosen it up a bit. There is no point in making pictures that you can't enter into imaginatively.

Remember the section on skies, in which we talked about graded tones. They are easy enough to create by dodging and burning-in and add a lot of depth to pictures. Graded tones are like highways into space. We grade the sky in a picture to make it look look like a real one: deep, deep, deep.

When we talked about corners we considered the tunnel effect, which is also a fast highway into the distance. Actually, the tunnel is just a special way of using tonal gradation.

You've already seen how contrast can be locally created or diminished. This knowledge can be used in depth manipulation to either increase or diminish it. In our everyday world there is a hierarchy of contrasts among things that are at various distances from us. We can use the same hierarchy in our prints. The way it works is that the closer things are to us the more they stand out (contrast). So in our prints we create contrast gradients, things that are near standing out, things at a middle distance standing out much less, and distant things nearly disappearing in their surroundings. We infrequently need to create a whole hierarchy, but we often need the knowledge for just one thing in a picture, either pushing it forward with high contrast or back with low contrast.

We mustn't forget the ancient "stepping-stone trick," which is still as good as it ever was. The idea is that the eye moves back into picture space by jumping from tone to tone as if they were stepping stones in a stream. So we add some extra tones to a picture to give the eye extra things to jump from, thus creating a stronger illusion of depth. The eye actually doesn't work this way, but the trick is very effective anyway.

The tone areas that we add don't have to be sharply defined. In fact it is better if they aren't, because they might be too obtrusive; they will create the depth illusion even if people don't notice them. It is easiest to use the trick on landscapes. For example, imagine a picture mostly filled with a vast expanse of sand or grass. Let's say that the space is flatly lighted and that the picture itself looks flat. By dodging, we can put in two or three strips of lighter tone, which will work as stepping stones even though they are long. With most pictures of this sort they would add considerably to the depth.

Totally dodging one side of the face created this unusual effect.

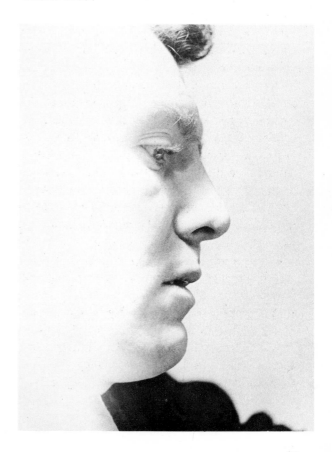

● Get the Basic Print First

Now that you've had a taste of the things that can be done by dodging and burning-in you are probably all hot to try them. They are lots of fun, friend, no doubt of that, but slow down. Slow 'way, 'way down. If you start your messing around too soon you'll never get things sorted out right.

Always start out working from the best-possible basic print: remember, it has the right contrast, the right exposure, and the right processing.

One eye and its side of the face were dodged considerably. The other eye was burned-in to make it look like a black hole in the face.

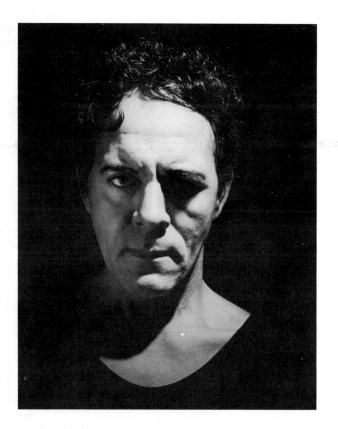

Except for needing local manipulation it is beyond improvement. If you start with a print like this it is easy to tell what your dodging and burning-in are, or are not, contributing to it. However, if you start with a sloppy work print you'll never know which is doing what to whom. And it is like a great chef spending all day frosting a stale cake. The excellence of the frosting (dodging and burning-in) won't compensate for the worms in the cake (a bad basic print).

● Use Your Crystal Ball

The dodging and burning-in techniques you have just read about are not golden keys to everything whatever. They can only serve as guidelines or as clues concerning the kinds of things to look for in pictures. Therefore, look at your pictures through your crystal ball and psych your own way into seeing where and how the various tricks might apply. They work very well, you may be sure, but only if you *make* them work.

Consider the paragraphs in this chapter as puzzles, if you wish, for that may help them engage your attention. For example, you might ask yourself, "Why will lightening the tops of things and darkening their bottoms sometimes loosen up a picture and give it a strong feeling of depth?" Don't pretend you know already, for you most assuredly don't. You have to work it out by trial and error in printing. When you think you have the answer, ask yourself, "When will *darkening* the tops of things and *lightening* their bottoms do the very same things?"

Don't settle for verbal answers, which are mainly useless in photography. Answer yourself with your prints—no other way. Though this is a book for beginners, a good deal of artistic knowledge was compressed in this chapter. Don't be fooled by the fact that it read like instructions for assembling a Yo-yo. Knowledge can be concealed in simplicity, you know.

HOW TO SPOT AND RETOUCH PRINTS

No matter how well you clean your negatives, your prints will almost always have a few dust spots and hair squiggles on them, anyway. It's just one of those things we have to put up with in photography. The white spots and squiggles are unsightly, of course, so we have to get rid of them. We do this by dye spotting or retouching, which actually mean the same thing. However, "spotting" is usually associated with just dust spots and squiggles, "retouching" with more extensive repairs.

The theory is simple: blemishes caused by dust or lint on negatives stand out on prints because they are white. Ergo, we put dye in them, just enough to match the surrounding areas in tone. This makes the blemishes disappear without a trace.

We don't have to limit ourselves to dust spots and squiggles, however. There can be many other things that need to be either removed entirely or toned down. For example, in a landscape foreground we might want to get rid of paper scraps or pop bottles. In a portrait there might be an unsightly spot of light on the subject's collar. Or we may have a lovely beach picture spoiled by cigarette packages. Such things can be de-emphasized or eliminated.

Things can be altered in other ways. Say Aunt Maud's nose looks too long: it can be shortened. We don't like the white patch of skin above Albert's sock: we put dye in it, making the sock look longer. An area in a picture looks too empty: we add some extra tones to it with dye. The list of things you can do with dyes is almost endless, so if you like this kind of thing (some don't) you will find lots to amuse you.

● Things You Need

Sable spotting brush
Black Spotone dye (no. 3)—or a three-color kit
Small tube of white water color or gouache
White saucer
Eye dropper
Paper towels or napkins
Q-Tips or surgical cotton
Photo-Flo or dishwashing detergent
Magnifying glass
An envelope flap with mucilage on it
Pieces of photographic blotter

● Your Work Light

To spot prints you need good light, or you won't be able to see the tip of your brush against the darker areas of your print. This leads to missing the dust spots and getting dye in all the wrong places, which will really make a mess of a print. Work near a brightly lit window or under a 150-watt bulb about two feet away. Some people hate to spot, mainly because they can't see what they are doing. Don't let it happen to you.

If you do wreck a print, don't worry. Putting it in a tray of water for a while will wash out most of the dye. If you need to get rid of more, put it in hypo, then wash and dry it as usual. It is better to do this than tear up your print and scream bloody murder, as some people do.

● Use a Magnifier or a Reading Glass

Seeing what you are doing is so important that you may need a magnifier, even if your close-up vision is excellent and the light is strong. You need it most when you are working on thin lines from backing scratches or hairs, which are very difficult to spot without slopping the dye over onto surrounding areas. When magnified sufficiently they look as wide as sidewalks and are quite easy to spot—like parking a tricycle in a four-car garage. Follow this general rule: before you try to spot something make sure you can see it.

● Overcoming the Gelatin

If the artists of the world congregated to pick the type of surface most difficult to work on, their unanimous choice would be gelatin—and we photographers are stuck with it. Of all the things to have to put dye on evenly: photographic Jell-O! But when a print needs spotting there is no running away from it, so we have to do the best we can. There are a couple of little tricks that help, however.

The first is to put a few drops of Photo-Flo (or dishwashing detergent) in the water you work with. It flattens out those little round drops of dye that always sink into a print at the wrong time and place. It also makes it easier to lay smooth dye tones down on fairly large areas, up to an inch or two.

Another trick is to dampen local areas just before you work on them. They should be cold and a little soft but free of surface water. Damp gelatin takes dye quickly and smoothly, which can

hardly be said of it when it is dry. Some people prefer to do their spotting fairly soon after processing, when their prints still aren't fully dry. They spot them first, dry them later. If you stack prints on top of each other they'll stay damp for quite a while, and it does them no harm.

Your own tongue can help you overcome the recalcitrance of dry gelatin, which doesn't want to accept dye at all. Instead of wetting your brush with water, lick it. There is just enough stickiness in saliva for it to help dye stick to the most obstinate print. The dye is harmless.

There is a related trick that is possibly more aesthetic. Wet your brush in water, stroke it a few times across the mucilage on an envelope flap, then pick up the dye with it. It doesn't work better than saliva, but it works.

There are some patient people who get a tremendous charge out of dye retouching and do a lot of it. They generally like to use non-hardening hypo, which is mixed with only hypo crystals and none of the other ingredients of an acid-hardening fixing bath. One would use about the same weight of crystals as the mixed dry chemicals (twenty-five ounces per gallon) This non-hardening fixer leaves the gelatin a little softer, less rubbery, and more acceptant of the dye—but more vulnerable too, so you have to treat it with care! Mainly you should be wary of your own fingernails.

The non-hardening hypo is all right with regular papers of all brands, though some are more fragile than others. But there are some brands of resin-coated (RC) paper that really *have* to be hardened. If not, the emulsions get as sticky as glue, get scratched at the merest touch, or slide right off the plastic base. Kodak RC papers are all right, however, so you should stick with them. Even so, you should wash and dry the prints right after processing and handle them carefully while spotting. When spotting a non-hardened print of any kind it is a good idea to lay typing paper on the part your hand will rest on. Very good protection from rings, bracelets, watch bands, and fingernails. Mostly fingernails.

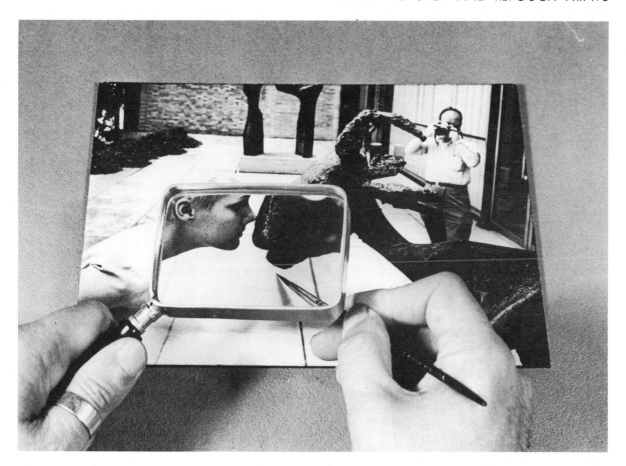

• Setting Up Your Saucer

You will use a white saucer for your palette and should prepare it in advance. Put about six or eight drops of Spotone near one edge. Across from it squeeze out about half an inch of white water color or gouache (they're about the same thing). Let them dry thoroughly. This concentrates the dye considerably, so that you can make very black dots and lines with it. It doesn't concentrate the white but makes it easier to control the amount that you get on your brush, which can be quite important. These amounts of black and white should last you for months without your adding to them.

When you are ready to use your saucer, put a match folder under one side so that you can confine a puddle of water to the other without its running into either the dye or the water color.

Print spotting is easy if you use a strong reading glass.

Lay a paper napkin or towel next to the saucer. Put a glass of water near the napkin and add a little Photo-Flo to it (eight or ten drops). Drop some water into the saucer to make your "working puddle."

• Loading and Pointing Your Brush

Spotting is much easier if you load (fill or wet) and point your brush properly. If you dip it in a glass of water you usually load it too full, which is why we use the little puddle on the saucer: one can pick up small amounts of water from the edge of it. The next step is to pick up some dye, the amount depending on the tone of the area you are spotting. Against the white of the saucer, you can easily see the concentration of the dye and increase or decrease it according to your needs.

When the brush has dye in it, it may be too heavily loaded and need to be pointed. If so, use the napkin to take up the excess dye. Hold the brush almost parallel to the table and stroke the point on the napkin two or three times, or until the load seems about right. This will also give it a needle-sharp point.

If you need a slightly stickier mixture you can wet and point the brush with your lips, sometimes before you pick up dye with it, sometimes afterward. Your lips and the napkin are equally good for controlling the amount of dye.

When you are through spotting you should carefully point the brush with your lips and put it where nothing will touch the point and warp it out of shape. However, if it does get bent, load it with undiluted white water color, shape it, and let it dry. When you wash it out the point will be all right again.

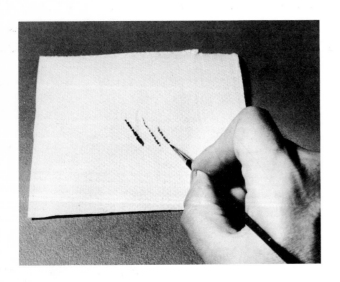

In print spotting, it is important to keep the brush sharply pointed and to control the amount of dye in it. You can do both by stroking it on a paper napkin or towel.

• Brush Patterns

Unless it is very small, don't try to fill a dust spot with just one touch of the brush, for if you do you will probably get too much dye in it. Dye sinks right into the gelatin and isn't that easy to get out. So fill in the larger spots bit by bit with little dots of dye. If the spots resist the dye, as they often do, use a little mucilage or saliva in your brush. *Don't* try to solve the problem by using a too heavily loaded brush.

To fill in white lines and hair marks, use a magnifier or a reading glass. Don't try to fill one in with a single stroke, or you will surely make a mess of it. Instead, use a lot of short lines or little dots. It isn't necessary to eliminate lines and hair marks the first time, for you can go over them several times if necessary. And it is safer to do it this way.

If at any time you lay too much dye down, wipe it up *immediately* with the napkin or your fingertip. Otherwise, you'll be stuck with it.

• Dyeing Larger Areas

No matter what we do to make gelatin a better surface to work on we can't make it take dye very evenly. We can improve matters a bit, but that is all. Thus you shouldn't try something like darkening a clear sky, because the results will look like a finger painting by a distracted monkey. This will always happen if you chose large areas of smooth, or even, tone. You can sometimes handle small smooth-tone areas, however.

It is best to restrict yourself to areas with texture in them, the more random the better. It will help cover up the mistakes you make with the dye.

To cover larger areas (one to two inches) use a brush heavily loaded with very heavily diluted dye. Put the dye on very wet, then *immediately* blot it with a photographic blotter, pressing down firmly. Repeat this process until the tone is just right.

For somewhat smaller areas, use a Q-Tip.

Load it with dye so diluted that it has hardly any color, then take off the excess by rolling it on a paper napkin. It should be just damp, so that the dye won't come off it in droplets. Rub the Q-Tip across a selected area until it is the right tone. Since the moisture will soften the gelatin, take care not to rub too hard.

There is a problem with spotting dyes: they often change color when they sink into gelatin, usually turning brown or blue. Residual hypo in the emulsion may be the cause. Most of the time, the colors are invisible against the neutral tones of a print. However, if you use too much dye, apply it in too large an area, or both, the color will stand out like carnal sin. You should therefore consider dye retouching as a way of making moderate changes in prints, not dramatic ones. And when you darken sizable areas you are doing something that could be done better by burning-in, though this is not always true.

If you already have a color problem with a retouched print, you might buy the blue and brown Spotone dyes (or start out with the three-color kit). The blue will more or less neutralize a brown on your print, and the brown neutralize a blue.

• Using the White Water Color

The white is obviously used for things that need lightening instead of darkening, but we have to use it conservatively. The reason is that the water color doesn't have the same surface sheen as the print, so that it stands out too much when the print is viewed from certain angles. However, if we use it on very small things—black spots and squiggles—it won't be too obvious, at least not as obvious as the defects themselves would be.

What we usually need in our spotting is a gray tone, not white, because the area surrounding the defect is usually a tone of gray. You can mix a gray by combining the water color with your dye, but that is not the best way. Instead, get your gray by using the white in very small amounts. Some of the dark tone underneath it will show

through, making it look gray. To load your brush, liberally wet it with your lips, then stroke it once or twice across the dried water color on the saucer. This will give you a very thin white mixture.

• Other Things You Can Do with Dye and Water Color

1. Add texture to things that need it.
2. Sharpen the edges of out-of-focus things.
3. Change facial expression by working on the corners of the mouth, nose creases, and eyes.
4. Separate things that blend too much.
5. Blend things that separate too much.
6. Fill in straggly hair.
7. Put highlights in eyes (with white) or reshape existing highlights (usually with dye alone).
8. Add detail to washed-out areas.
9. Modify the shapes of things.
10. Paint in grass, leaves, twigs, etc.
11. Strengthen weak lines and edges.
12. Even out skin blemishes somewhat.
13. Clean up the contours of things.
14. Emphasize important centers of interest.
15. Subordinate distracting areas.

It would be helpful for you to think of dye retouching as an extension of burning-in. They are often interchangeable, so that the things that can be done by burning-in can also be done (to some degree) be retouching, and vice versa.

• Take Your Time

In your first efforts at print spotting and retouching, you may feel compelled to work rapidly, with verve and dash. Don't do it! For speed is the road to catastrophe. Work *very* slowly and carefully. With a little practice you will find that you can move along like a sleepy turtle and still retouch as many as fifteen prints per hour, which is making haste slowly. So be patient and take your time. Don't pretend to yourself that you already know how to use a brush; you don't. That too will take a little time.

HOW TO IMPROVE PRINTS BY BLEACHING

One of the photographer's favorite creative tools is an easily prepared bleach made of potassium ferricyanide and water. It can also be made with hypo instead of water and is then called "Farmer's reducer," after the man who invented it. The water solution is more convenient, however, because it doesn't deteriorate quite as rapidly. Farmer's will work only for fifteen to twenty minutes before it must be discarded and remixed.

If you have made prints that came out too dark you can appreciate the value of a chemical that will lighten them to any desired degree. Though bleaching won't save all overexposed prints, it will resurrect enough of them to make it worth using. Very inexpensive in itself, it can save you a lot of money on printing paper.

Salvaging an overcooked print is just one of the handy things that bleach can do. You can also lighten selective areas in a print with it, using it as a kind of chemical dodger. If you forget to dodge an area during exposure or don't dodge it enough, you can use bleach to lighten it as much as you think necessary, even to the point of eliminating it altogether. Furthermore, with "bleach dodging" you can work on a dozen areas in a given print, which you just don't have time for with regular dodging. During a ten-second exposure, for example, you couldn't use a single dodging tool to dodge twelve different areas for five seconds each. However, they can be "dodged" (lightened) with bleach later.

Bleach is also used for "cutting out," or cleaning up, white backgrounds, which means reducing them to a pristine white. This is most often done with skies and walls, but you can whiten anything you like. Bleach can be used in print retouching for eliminating dark spots and lines, removing beer cans from scenic pictures, sharpening out-of-focus edges, lightening bags under eyes, eliminating pimples or scars, lightening the whites of eyes, brightening facial highlights, and so on.

Used as a team, bleaching (lightening) and dye retouching (darkening) will in some degree do all the things that dodging (lightening) and burning-in (darkening) do together, including adding space to prints, increasing or decreasing local contrast, emphasizing or subordinating centers of interest, etc.

In terms of what they can do for pictures it is useful to think of bleaching and dodging as being about the same thing. Similarly, dyeing and burning-in are much alike.

● Things You Need

Potassium ferricyanide: A fairly poisonous red-orange crystalline compound; don't get it in your mouth or eyes. In a water or hypo solution, it will bleach metallic silver.

Hypo: One can use an ordinary acid-hardening fixing bath, a rapid fixer, or simply hypo crystals in water. Use the fixer that is already in your print-processing line.

Glass or cup: A six-ounce glass or a white teacup are about the right size, because you will be mixing bleach in four-ounce quantities; it is economical that way.

Measuring spoons: Should be plastic so they won't react with the ferricyanide when you are measuring it out.

Photo-Flo: You will add five drops to each four-ounce batch of bleach. It prevents the bleach from forming little droplets, which lighten areas where they touch the print much too rapidly, making small, round white spots that require dye spotting.

Eye dropper: Buy one at a drugstore. Better yet, get half a dozen, as they are very handy.

A no. 4 sable brush: Sable only—never camel's hair or a synthetic—for precision bleaching of small areas and working around contours of all

Equipment and chemicals for bleaching include a print-inspection board, potassium ferricyanide, Photo-Flo, brush, eye dropper, Q-Tip, cotton, sponge, fixer, and a brush.

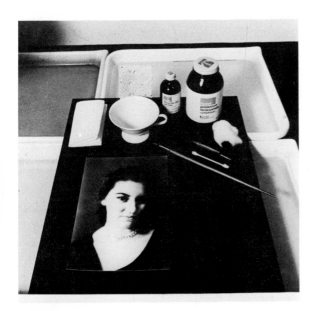

sizes and shapes. Before buying a brush, wet it with your lips to see that it makes a good point; some don't. Unsanitary but practical.

Clear nail polish: For sealing the brush ferrule against bleach, thus preventing blue stains (see Dektol, below). Wet the brush, point it with your lips, and let it thoroughly dry. Then give the ferrule two or three coats of nail polish, letting each coat dry before you apply the next one. Next put a tiny drop of it on the brush hairs at the point where they disappear into the ferrule. The lacquer should seep into the hairs, sealing off the *inside* of the ferrule from the bleach. If the brush isn't sealed, the iron in the ferrule (especially the inside) will react with the ferricyanide to form a blue stain.

Surgical cotton and Q-Tips: For applying bleach to prints.

Print-inspection board or tray bottom: Lay it right across the stop-bath tray, next to the first hypo, and make sure that the hypo light strikes it squarely. It should be a sturdy arrangement, so that you don't splash bleach all over everything including your Sunday clothes.

Ordinary viscose sponge: Prior to bleaching, prints are soaked in hypo. The sponge is for removing most of it when the print is on the inspection board, just before you start working on it. It is also for containing hypo to slow down the bleaching action in areas being treated.

Paper towels: For removing all the rest of the surface hypo (even the *tiniest* droplets) from the print just before bleaching (by itself, a sponge just won't remove enough of the hypo). Folded twice, a fresh paper towel is used as a blotter to rapidly slow down bleaching action so it won't get out of control.

Hypo light: As in dye retouching, one needs a strong work light in order to see where the brush tip is touching the print.

Magnifier or reading glass: Needed for bleaching such things as small black spots or thin black lines. Without one, you can't guide your brush accurately and will get bleach on the areas surrounding the defects you wish to lighten.

Tray: For containing a quart of solution when you wish to bleach an entire print at one time. Either an 8×10 or an 11×14 tray will do nicely.

Dektol: If there is iron or rust in your water supply you may get blue stains on your prints, either as over-all tints or as small, intensely blue spots. If you put them in Dektol, which won't harm them a bit, the stains will usually go away. Afterward, acidify them in stop bath, reharden in hypo, then wash and dry as usual. This treatment will not change their tones one iota, but it nearly always gets rid of the blue.

• Strength of Bleach Solutions

Most photographers mix bleach by eye, judging its strength by how yellow it is. Thus a weak bleach is a light lemon yellow, a strong one dark yellow. Using a white cup, you can see the color well. However, at this point in your experience you don't really know how yellow the yellow should be, so we will use some simple recipes, with bleach crystals measured in fractions of a level teaspoonful.

For bleaching all parts of a print at once, use one-eighth teaspoonful of ferricyanide per quart of water. This will give you a moderately dilute solution that is safe to work with, because it won't bleach too fast. It can also be used for local bleaching where little lightening is required.

For bleaching local areas you can work with stronger solutions, mixed in four-ounce quantities. In using them the main problem (a serious one) is to not let the bleaching action get away from you, thus ruining the print. However, stronger solutions save a lot of time.

To four ounces of water add five drops of Photo-Flo and one of the following quantities of potassium ferricyanide crystals:

Medium-strong – ¹⁄₁₆ teaspoonful
Strong – ⅛ teaspoonful
Ultra-strong – ¼ to ½ teaspoonful

Until you have had a lot of experience with bleach, you should stick mainly to the medium-strong, using the strong rarely and avoiding the ultra-strong altogether. Unless you know your stuff the ultra-strong will simply get away from you. However, you won't really believe this until you have ruined a few prints with it, so feel free to experiment.

Unfortunately, your measuring spoons go down only to one fourth of a teaspoon. To get an idea of what one eighth of a spoon of crystals looks like, measure out one-fourth teaspoonful, put it on a piece of paper, and divide the pile in half. Divide one of the halves to get one sixteenth. When you have an approximate idea of what the quantities look like it is safe enough to guess them. As you see, it takes only small amounts to make rather strong solutions.

• Factors Affecting Speed of Bleaching

You will soon see that the fine art of print bleaching can't be learned overnight. You have to practice and you have to get used to the uncertain behavior of bleach solutions. One of the problems is that you can never predict how fast they will work on a given print. However, the speed-affecting factors are known.

Freshly mixed solutions work *much* faster than ones that have sat around for a while, even for ten minutes or so. Minerals in your water supply, and hypo that gets into the bleach solution, gradually form compounds with the ferricyanide, slowing it down until it finally won't bleach at all.

Light areas in prints bleach *much* faster than darker ones. At least, the fact that they get lighter is much more obvious, which is the same thing for practical purposes.

Naturally, strong bleach solutions work more rapidly than weak ones.

The print-developing time is an important factor. The less time you give a print the faster it will bleach. In prints developed one minute or less, the light areas bleach very rapidly, the medium and dark areas fairly rapidly. In two-minute prints the light areas bleach at a moderate rate, medium areas slowly, and dark areas very slowly. In five-minute prints only the light areas are affected at all by bleach, unless one uses a very strong solution.

Bleach applied very wet works much faster than a thin coat of it. Thus it works slowly when applied with a squeezed-out cotton wad or a brush that is damp rather than well loaded.

• Over-all Bleaching

We use over-all bleaching on prints that are overexposed but normally developed. They are thus too dark, but bleaching can often bring them back to normal tones of good quality. Prints overexposed up to 100 per cent (one stop) can usually be saved, but the less overexposure the better. Sometimes you can even rescue prints that are as much as two stops over, but you shouldn't count on it.

If overexposed prints are also *underdeveloped* the bleach will often cause a disagreeable, mottled effect. Therefore, if you see a print coming up too fast in the developer, don't "jerk" it, but let it remain in the tray for about 1½ minutes. It will be much too dark, of course, yet you *may* be able to save it by bleaching. If you jerk a print you might as well kiss it good-by.

If only half of a print is too dark, as often happens, put only that half in the bleach, moving it around so that the bleaching action will be even. Be careful not to get bleach on the part you are keeping out of the tray.

Over-all bleaching is also used to give prints extra "snap" and to increase contrast up to one paper contrast grade. To increase contrast, over-expose the print about 20 per cent, develop it from 2 to 2½ minutes, then bleach it. In a print developed this long the darks won't bleach very much while the light areas will, thus increasing the "tonal distance" (contrast) between them. Essentially, giving a print more snap means to increase the contrast a bit.

• Over-all Bleaching Step by Step

1. Pour half a capful of Photo-Flo into a quart of water, stir it, then add one-eighth teaspoonful (level measure) of potassium ferricyanide crystals. Stir until the crystals are completely dissolved. This is very important.

2. Soak your print thoroughly in the fixing bath.

3. Pour the bleach in a tray and put the print in it.

4. Immediately start rocking the tray in an irregular way, so that the bleach flows over the print in a random pattern.

5. After ten seconds remove the print, drain it three seconds, and put it in the hypo, agitating for ten seconds or more.

6. Examine the print under the hypo light to see how much it has been bleached.

7. If more bleaching is needed, drain the print and return it to the bleach tray. If there was very little bleaching action the first time, you can safely increase the time to to twenty seconds, provided that the print is still quite obviously too dark. Then return it to the hypo and agitate as before. This process can be repeated many times, if necessary.

Doing it in stages this way is the best method for holding the bleaching action under control. If you try to bleach a print all the way the first time it is in the bleach bath, you will probably ruin it. One reason is that you will develop a compulsion to watch it bleach until it has gone too far. Another is that some of the bleaching goes on after the print goes into the hypo. Thus a print that looks just right in the bleach bath may end up being too light after the hypo has worked on it. This is why we inspect prints in the hypo, not the bleach.

After bleaching, fix the print thoroughly (for twice the time it takes for the yellow stain to disappear), then wash and dry it as usual.

The small amount of bleach that normally gets carried over into the fixing bath will neither harm it nor turn it into an effective Farmer's reducer solution. You can safely run other prints through it. However, if you dump a *lot* of bleach into it, you may have to test its bleaching action and possibly discard it. If you drain each print for three seconds after bleaching it, you should be able to work all day without harming the fixer.

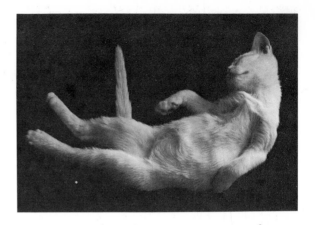

For over-all bleaching, the print is both overexposed and overdeveloped (above). The bleach lightens the whole print somewhat (below), especially the highlights, which bleach much faster than darker tones.

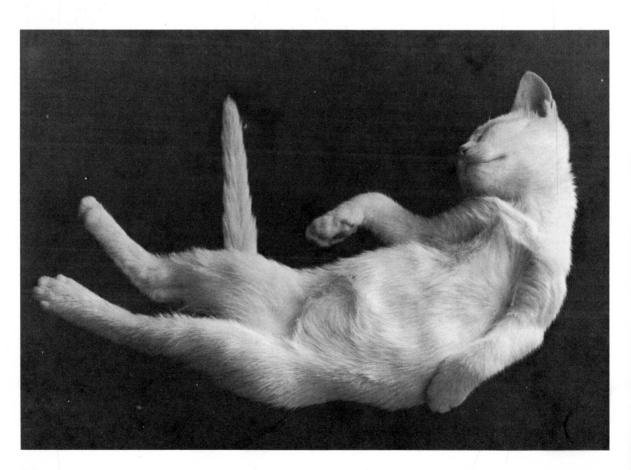

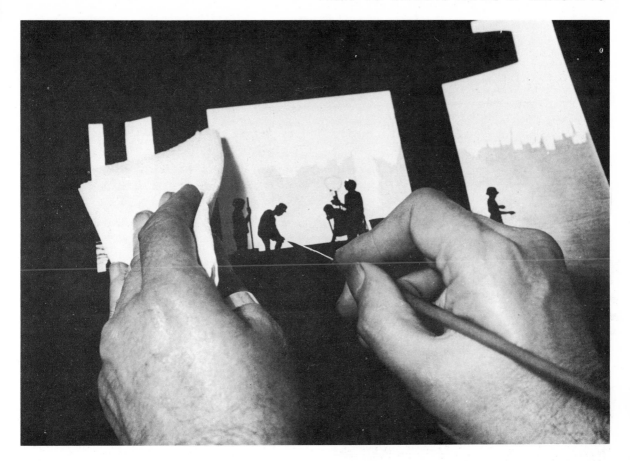

Working by the bleach-and-blot method on a print whose surface has been wiped thoroughly dry. Bleach is applied, then immediately blotted with a paper napkin. This stops it from bleaching too far or spreading. It is one of the main control methods used in print bleaching.

● **Local Bleaching Step by Step**

1. Put five drops of Photo-Flo into four ounces of water, stir, then add one-sixteenth teaspoonful of bleach crystals, stirring until they are completely dissolved. For stirring, you can use a small stick, a Q-Tip, or a teaspoon made of plastic or stainless steel.

2. Soak your print thoroughly in the fixing bath. It works somewhat better if the print has just been made and never dried.

3. Lay out your print-inspection board under the hypo light, next to the hypo tray. Near its top edge place the cup of bleach, the brush, a Q-Tip, a wad of cotton, the sponge, and two paper towels —one of them folded twice to serve as a blotter.

4. Drain the print, lay it on the board (or tray bottom), and wipe it thoroughly with the sponge (which has been soaked in hypo, then squeezed out).

5. Wipe the print even more thoroughly with a paper towel, so that even the *tiniest* droplets are gone.

6. Wet the brush, then point it and remove the excess bleach by stroking it on the first paper towel.

7. While holding the folded paper towel in your left hand, apply some bleach to the print and *immediately* blot it *dry* with the towel. Wait about

ten seconds for the hypo that is still in the emulsion to carry the bleaching action forward.

8. Inspect the area to determine how much bleaching occurred, then repeat the bleach-and-blot procedure as many times as necessary. *Never wait to see what the bleach is doing, but blot first and find out later. Waiting to see is a sure road to ruin.*

9. After every two or three bleach-and-blots, put some hypo on the area with a sponge, so that the continuing action of the bleach will be carried through to its end. It is also good to return the print to the hypo bath now and then—for the same reason.

10. If the area still needs bleaching, wipe off the print as before and continue with the bleaching and blotting.

11. When the print has bleached sufficiently, put it in the hypo for twice the time it takes the yellow stain (caused by the ferricyanide) to disappear.

12. Wash it and dry it as usual.

These lengthy instructions are designed to spell out the controls for you, line by line. However, print beaching isn't necessarily a slow and tedious process unless you intend to do a lot of it on a given print. Just lightening an area here and there can be a matter of only a few seconds.

The slight bags under the eye in A can be fairly easily removed by bleaching, but pronounced ones would be very difficult to handle. In detail B we see what happens when one gets impatient and used bleach that is too strong. It could be spotted with dyes, but it would take several laborious hours. Print C shows the image after a conservative amount of bleaching.

A

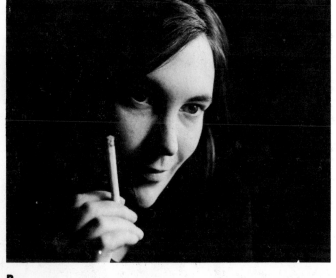

B

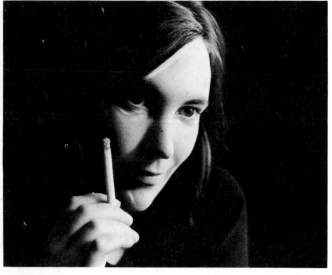

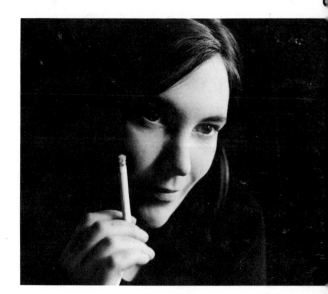

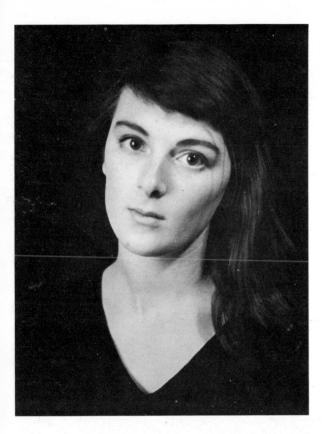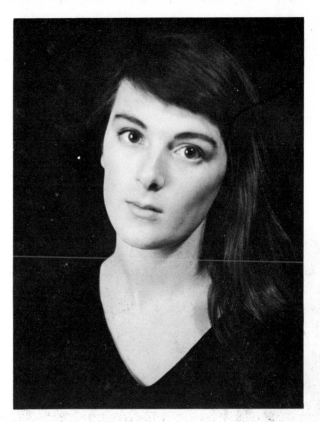

In print at left the hair shadows and neck wrinkles are a little unsightly, though the rest of the picture is all right. They were bleached out in print at right with moderately strong bleach and the bleach-and-blot method. In working on such fine details as this you should always work with a magnifying glass so that you can see where the brush point is touching the print.

● Haste Makes Waste

Though lightening a few areas may take little time, extensive bleach retouching and cutting out white backgrounds may be time-consuming and tedious. After working for perhaps twenty minutes on a print, impatience may set in and one may try to hurry things up by cutting out the print-wiping steps and using very strong bleach. You might as well know right now that this will almost invariably lead to disaster.

● A Fast-Cutting Print

If you know in advance that you are going to cut out a medium- or light-gray area, make a fast-cutting print. That is, overexpose and underdevelop it somewhat. For most papers, work for a developing time of one minute; with Kodak resin-coated (RC) papers you are usually safe in going as low as forty-five seconds. However, in both cases there will be a loss of contrast, so you should use a paper contrast grade or filter one step higher than you normally would.

When underdeveloping papers, slide them into the developer with one swift movement and maintain constant and erratic (random) agitation. Otherwise you may run into a problem with mottled tones.

You will find that the bleach works fast on prints of this type and that all areas—light, medium, and dark—are affected by it. Thus if you

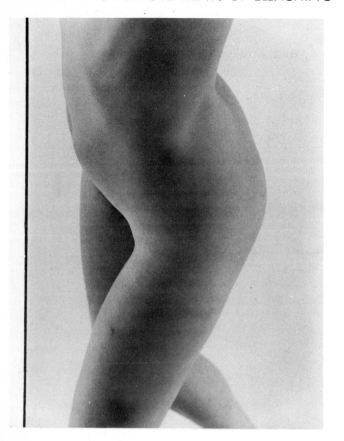

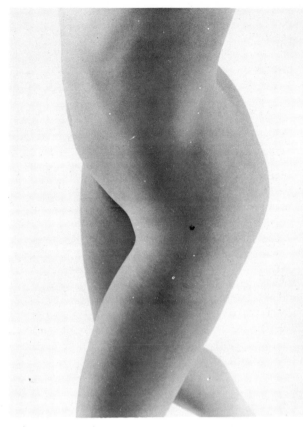

In print at left the background is a little dingy and the edge of the frame comes too close to the torso. In print at right the frame line has been dodged out and the rest of the background bleached out to a clean white.

do over-all bleaching in addition to working locally, use a very dilute or partly worn-out bleach.

• Bleach Turns Green

After it has been mixed for a while, bleach will turn green. If it is dilute the green is an indication that it is pretty well shot. However, strong bleaches can be as green as an emerald and still be very potent. The color won't get into your prints, so don't worry about it.

• Stains

You have already read about blue stains and how to deal with them, but you may also be troubled with yellow and brown stains. Either may be caused by insufficient time in the hypo, or using an exhausted hypo bath or too short a washing time.

Brown stains are often compounds of silver and ferricyanide, that is, silver that hasn't quite bleached all the way. If they fall in an area that you are cutting back to white you can generally get rid of them by alternating between strong bleach and hypo, if necessary even going to ultra-strong bleach. However, you must be careful in blotting the ultra-strong to keep it away from the rest of the image, for it will cut through tone like a knife.

Brown stains in areas that are supposed to remain medium or dark gray cannot be thus eliminated. However, they can be counteracted fairly well with light washes of blue spotting dry.

• Testing Bleaching Speed

Though the main factors influencing the speed of bleaching are known, one never knows for sure how fast a given print will bleach. If you test your bleach on light areas, it might get away from you even if it is a rather weak solution. You should therefore test it on medium or fairly dark tones, working your way gradually up to light ones.

If it should happen to work fast on medium tones you can be sure it would really clobber light ones. Thus it would be wise to dilute it considerably. On the other hand, if a bleach works too slowly, add more bleach crystals to it—but be sure to test the new mixture, too.

• Black Spots and Lines

Unless they fall in blank white areas, black spots and lines are a real agony to work on, because they take so long to disappear with medium or strong bleach, and it is so hard to keep the stuff out of adjacent areas. Though risky, it is sometimes best to turn to ultra-strong bleach. Use it in a carefully pointed *damp* brush, immediately blotting it and putting it into the hypo after each application. Remember that the ultra-strong brew is dynamite in itself, so don't take extra chances with it. However, if bleaching in areas as small as spots and lines goes a bit too far it can usually be patched up fairly easily by dye retouching—provided that you haven't slopped over into surrounding areas!

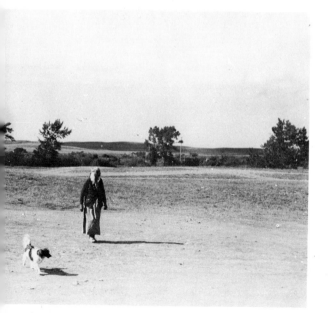 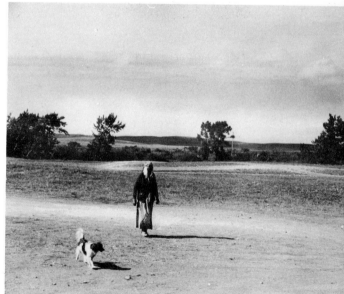

This picture of a Blackfoot Indian woman and her dog has a barren and empty feeling to it (left). In print at right the sky and foreground were burned-in and the whole picture made slightly darker. Then the lighter areas were created by bleaching.

You may find it fun to work with fast bleaches. If so, you should be willing to wipe out a few prints learning how to use the controls effectively. Work on pictures that don't quite make the grade, so you won't mind seeing them slide down the drain. But don't play fast on the draw with prints you really like.

• Keep It Moving

Sometimes it is safe to let bleach stand in an area awhile before blotting it. However, it will tend to draw into a puddle (even with Photo-Flo) so that the area isn't evenly covered. Thus the bleaching will be uneven. To counteract this, keep the bleach moving, going back and forth over the area with brush, cotton, or Q-Tip.

• Working Wet

If the edges of a lightened area don't have to be sharp, which is usually the case, you can often work on a print taken right out of the hypo and held in the palm of the left hand. Use medium-strong or strong bleach in a wad of cotton that has been well squeezed out. Blot your fingers so you won't get dribbles. After the print has drained four to five seconds, rub the area lightly with the cotton, but don't spend too long at it.

For a while, the squeezed-out cotton will simultaneously bleach the area it touches and absorb surface moisture, so that the bleach won't get loose into the surface hypo and get out of control.

After a few seconds, however, the cotton will get so full of hypo that it can't hold it any more. Along with the bleach it has picked up, the hypo will run amuck on the print. Thus when you use this method you should squeeze out the cotton again every two to three seconds, which prevents the rivulets. Though the technique sounds frightening it works well and very fast. Professional printers use it.

• You Know the Controls

The controls for successful print bleaching have been carefully spelled out so that you can start right out having fun with bleach. Many people find it one of the most fascinating tools of photography, and it could just as well be true for you.

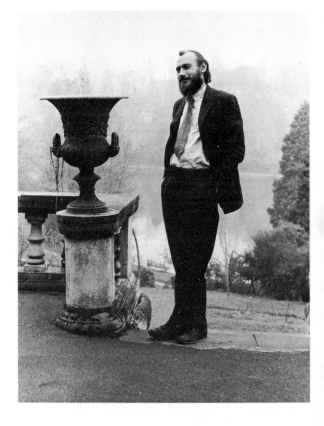

In print above the man's shirt is both dingy and wrinkled. Bleaching (right) improves it considerably. Notice that some of the wrinkles were left in; had they been entirely removed, the shirt would look like white plaster.

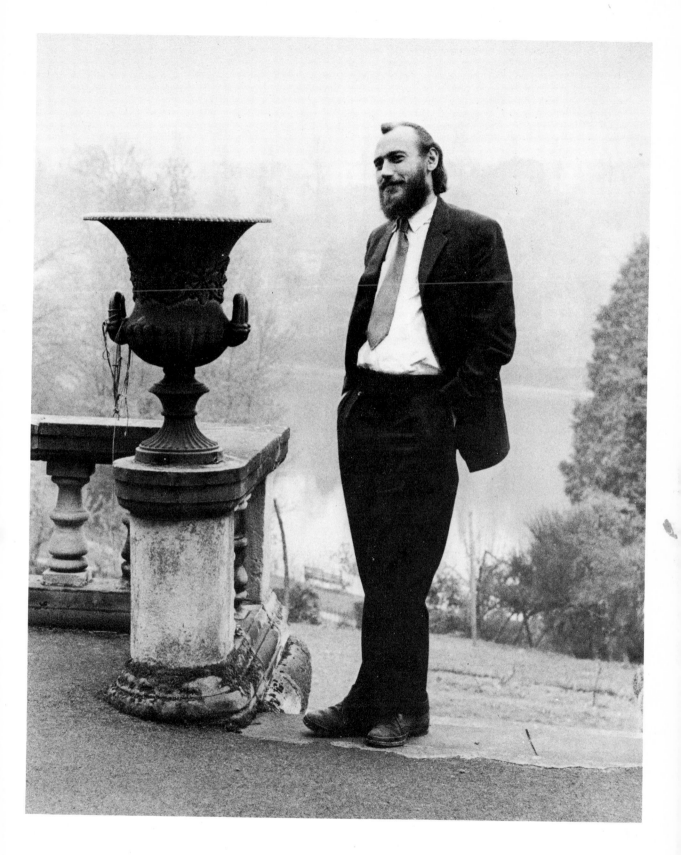

HOW TO MAKE MULTIPLE-IMAGE PRINTS FROM NEGATIVE SANDWICHES

It can be fascinating to create a multiple-image picture by printing more than one negative on a single piece of paper. Getting such an image is extremely easy, but it takes quite a bit of experimentation to come up with a really good one. Since the technique itself is so simple, you may not mind investing the materials and time required for top-notch results.

It is hard to say why we find multiple images so interesting. Perhaps it is because they are so strange; they surprise us, stimulating our minds and emotions. They tend to come across as pure symbolism, which is both unexpected and exciting. This may lead us to contemplate our personal symbolism and that which is universal, a useful step for better understanding of ourselves and others.

Frequently, multiple-image pictures have a strong resemblance to our dreams as we remember them. Indeed, for purposes of self-analysis or group discussion they can be dealt with as if they actually were dreams. The now-extensive psychology of dreams invariably fits multiple-image prints remarkably well.

However, your main motivation in working with this technique may be simply to surprise yourself as often as you can. This is as good a reason as any for playing with it.

● Things You Need

We will again use the list from page 65. Add to it the following:

Dodging and burning-in tools
Tools and materials for print bleaching

● The Basic Method

Instead of using just one negative at a time, "sandwich" (superimpose) two of them and make a print. Essentially, that is all there is to the method, though there are a few minor problems that should be dealt with.

● Picking the Negatives

The reasonable way to pick negatives is to think of all the pictures you have made and try to visualize how they would work together as multiple images. Reasonable, yes, but it just won't work. Things mentally visualized seldom work out until you have had a lot of experience.

You just have to wing it, but that is part of the fun. One way is to try all kinds of combinations of negatives in order to find ones that look good when held up to the light. The idea is that if sandwiches themselves look nice they will often make handsome pictures. On the other hand, some combinations that look unimpressive due to excessive density or flatness will make excellent prints, because these faults can be compensated for.

Beyond choosing sandwiches for their handsomeness or visual interest, the process is mainly a matter of trial and error. Some handsome superimpositions will print badly for unforeseeable reasons. And rather nondescript ones may make smashing prints. The only way to tell how a sandwich will print is to try it and find out. Since the art of photography was mainly developed by people who work this way, it would be educational for you to give it a try, too. If all it does is make you more philosophical about your mistakes in pictorial judgment, you will be a long way ahead. When you deal with the unpredictable, you should learn not to condemn your predictions.

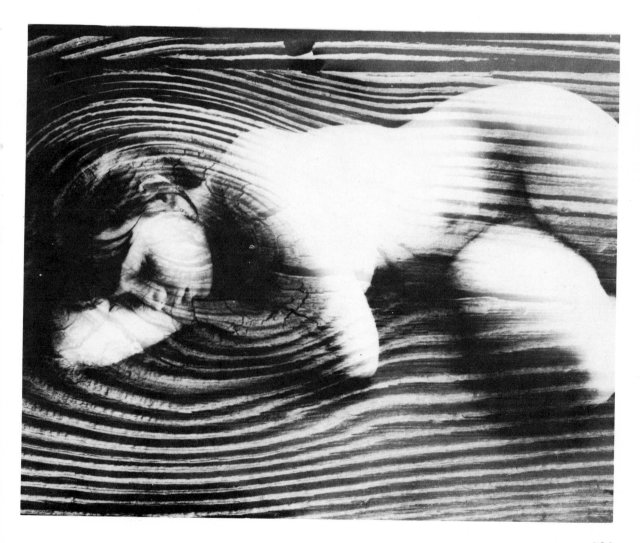

• Reversing Negatives, Flipping Them, and So On

From an innate sense of order and the rightness of things, you may feel that the two negatives in a sandwich should both be emulsion down, have their frames in register, and be oriented in the same direction from top to bottom. This would be unduly restricting yourself due to a false sense of pictorial piety. You can superimpose them this way if you like, but don't force yourself to stick to the formula. Since it is of the nature of multiple-image printing to commit mayhem on reality, you might as well add to the carnage just to see what happens.

Try sandwiching negatives emulsion to emulsion, back to back, top to bottom, and off register: you may get interesting results. You can pair negatives of two different sizes or sandwich a negative with a color slide (removed from its mount). Perhaps a fuzzy, out-of-focus negative would make a tasty sandwich when combined with a sharp one. See what you can think up, then give it a try.

• Cleaning Negatives

When you are printing a single negative, there are only two surfaces to collect dust. With sandwiched negatives there are four, so you should take great care in cleaning them (pages 44–48).

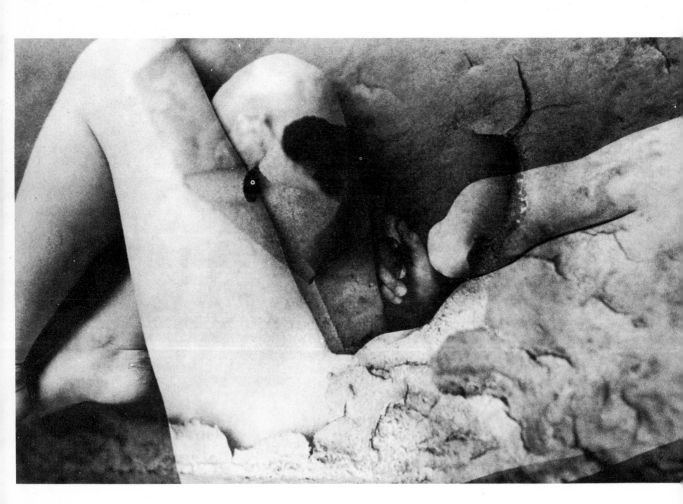

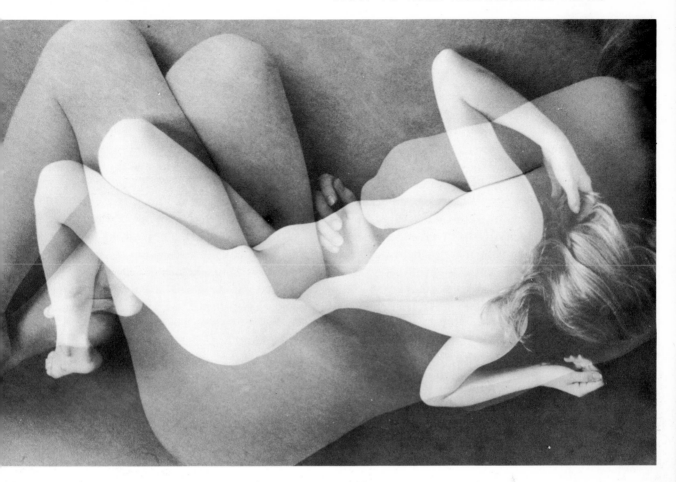

You should always clean negatives carefully, for that matter—unless you enjoy spending the lonely hours poking dye into dust spots on prints.

● Flatness and Contrast

Combined negatives often look very flat, because the light tones in one may neutralize the dark tones in the other. It can even go so far that a sandwich viewed against the light may look like a single solid expanse of gray.

Fortunately, the combinations aren't usually so totally lacking in contrast, though they lean in that direction. Most of the time, the flatness can be compensated for by using high-contrast paper or printing filters. For example, if the individual

negatives in a sandwich would print best on a no. 2 paper, the combination itself might be successfully printed on a no. 4. Thus, low contrast is not usually much of a problem.

Though most superimpositions tend toward flatness, not all of them do. Now and then, contrast is increased rather than decreased. It all depends on how the individual tones are overlapped. If the dark tones in one negative fall upon dark tones in the other, and if their light tones also overlap, there can be a considerable increase in contrast. Even so, such a sandwich will usually print well on an available contrast grade of paper (1 through 6). If it is even too contrasty for a no. 1, however, there are simple ways of flattening out the print as much as necessary (see the following chapter).

• The Density Problem

You will recall that the "density" of a negative refers to how dark it looks when viewed against a light source or brightly lit surface. It depends on both exposure and development, and there is an optimum density in what we call a "normal negative." However, when we sandwich two normal negatives we may double the optimum, depending on how the tones overlap. If they are "heavy" negatives (too dense) we get even more density.

Too much density in either a single negative or a sandwich can result in a slightly fuzzy print with mushy highlights. In the enlarger the excessive silver deposit acts as a diffuser, scattering some of the light as it passes through, making a print that seems slightly unsharp. Even with dense single negatives and superimpositions that are much too dense this doesn't always happen, however, so you should make test prints before rejecting them. If sandwiched negatives are both close to normal you should have no trouble with unsharpness.

Another problem with density is that it increases the print exposure time. Even with sandwiched normal negatives you will find yourself using exposure times ranging from thirty seconds to one or two minutes when the lens is stopped down three stops. You could cut the time by opening the lens, of course, but as you will see in a moment it isn't advisable. So you may be stuck with long exposure times. Though they stretch one's patience considerably, there is nothing wrong with long exposures per se. Indeed, pictures have been made with exposures lasting a whole day or two.

However, the time can lead to a problem with heat, which can warp negatives out of focus or even damage them. Thus you may have to print with prepopped negatives (or negative sandwiches) and break up long exposures into installments to allow the enlarger to cool. If you find the installments and cooling-off periods unduly tedious, read a book while you are waiting (with a darkroom-safe spotlight, which you can make by taping a five-inch cylinder of light cardboard or black paper to an ordinary flashlight).

• Stopping Down

The easiest way to sandwich two negatives is to position them both emulsion down, so they will curl together neatly like obedient spoons. Positioned emulsion to emulsion or back to back, their curl can make them as hard to handle as a greased pig. Thus if you have only the average amount of patience you will probably make most of your sandwiches the easy way.

This introduces a problem, however, in that the images on the two negatives are separated by one thickness of film base. Thus they are situated at different distances from both the lens and the printing paper, which simply means that when one image is sharp the other will be slightly out of focus—when the lens aperture is wide open for focusing. Fortunately, when we stop down three stops they will both be acceptably sharp. You can be sure of this if you focus *between* the images, rather than on one or the other. Though it sounds hard you will find it easy.

You can now see why we can't beat the problem of a long exposure time by simply opening up the lens. You may be safe in stopping down only twice, but don't count on it. With the lens wide open or stopped down only once the disparity in focus should be quite obvious. If you don't mind wrestling with a greased pig you can get around the problem by positioning the negatives emulsion to emulsion, because there will then be no separation at all between the images. However, you should stop down the lens a bit anyway, for it isn't sharp all the way to the edges at the larger aperture settings. But don't do it as a matter of rote, since some pictures look just fine with slightly soft edges.

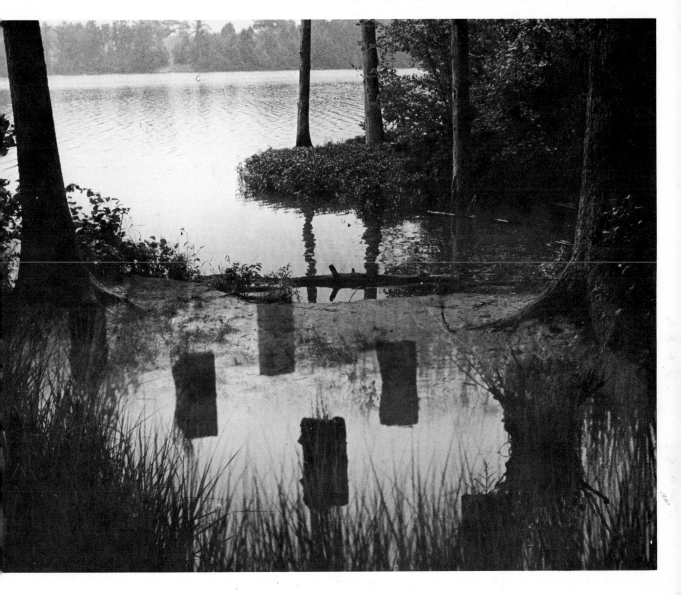

• Test Strips

When first using this unfamiliar technique, you should use an abundance of test strips and chips, both to determine exposures and to learn in the most economical way what sandwiching negatives does to prints. Since you will generally be working with heavier-than-usual densities, you can expect longer exposures, as we have seen. So increase the times for your test strips; for example, use the series 10–10–10 etc. seconds. For a very

dense sandwich, you could even use exposures of twenty or thirty seconds each.

• Dodging and Burning-In

In making multiple-image prints, you will often get dark tones where you want light ones, and vice versa, so make very liberal use of both dodging and burning-in. On account of the heavy densities, the burning-in times may be very long for certain prints. In such cases you may wish to dare the forbidden: open up the lens all the way for burning-in. With some pairs of negatives, there will be no tangible loss of quality; with others, there will be. You just have to try it and see.

You were told you should never dodge an area for more than 50 per cent of the exposure time, but this doesn't necessarily apply to printing negative sandwiches, especially if they are very dense. With the dense ones, you can sometimes dodge an area up to 80 per cent or more of the total time without its looking muddy or washed out.

• Bleaching

With multiple-image printing, you may wish to make more tone changes than you can handle with just dodging and burning-in, so wade into your prints with flourish and bleach.

• Dye Retouching

Don't forget that dyeing is an extension of burning-in; you may need it.

• Surprise!

Making multiple-image prints will probably turn out to be an emotional adventure for you, provided that you stick with it long enough to get a few passable images. Your ego will have a rough time, because it will predict numerous results that will fail to happen. Something else will always happen instead, for better or for worse. But giving your ego a hard time is the way to take the blinders off your eyes so that you can see better.

It would be wise to take the symbolism matter seriously, because this technique is a way of almost automatically bringing your hidden personal symbols to the surface, where you can see them. You will be pleased to see them, no doubt, but you are also likely to get shaken up a bit. It is like suddenly confronting yourself in a mirror in a darkened and unfamiliar house: shocking! Yet the experience will be good for you, because it will help you learn who you really are.

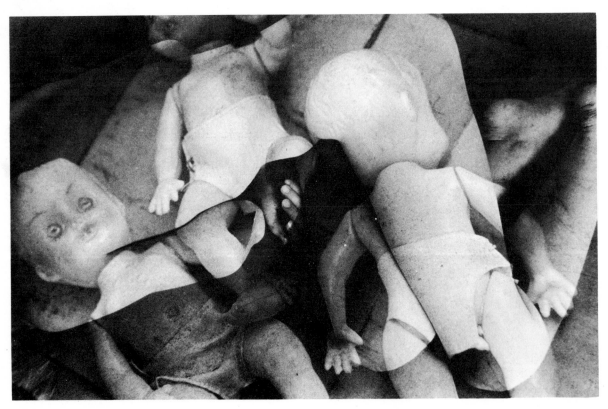

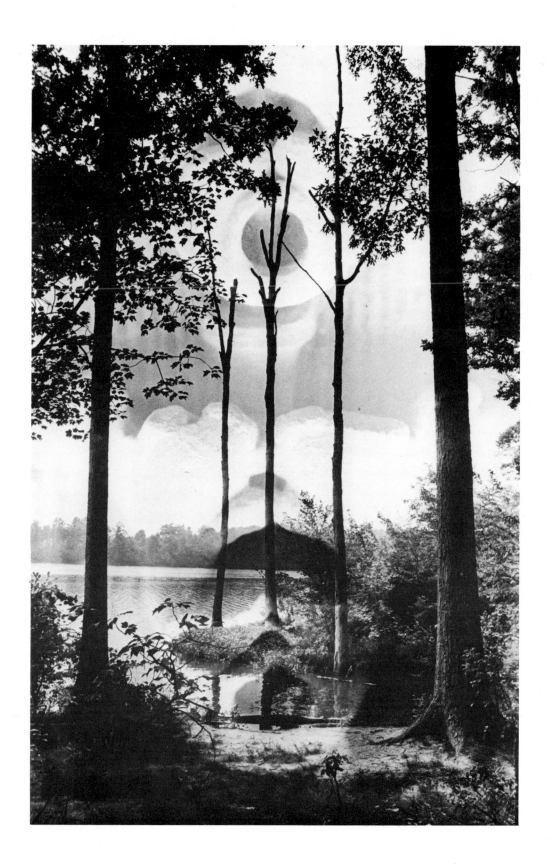

HOW TO CONTROL PRINT CONTRAST BY DEVELOPER DILUTION AND FLASHING

There are times when you may wish to reduce the contrast of a given paper as little as one contrast grade or as much as even four or five. There could be several reasons for this, for example when you have on hand only high-contrast paper and discover that your negatives require low-contrast ones. Or it may be that you can afford to buy only one package of paper, so you chose high-contrast, knowing that you can flatten it out if necessary. On the other hand, you may have negatives so contrasty that they would require a nonexistent grade of paper well below a no. 1, so you could start with a no. 1 and take it down to a minus 4 or 5.

Sometimes the reasons for flattening are strictly pictorial: you may want a print that is very flat, light, and delicate; and you can use a flattening technique not for contrast reduction as such but for bleaching, for reasons that will be explained later.

You will be given two excellent techniques, one involving intentional overexposure and underdevelopment, the other revolving around intentional *under*exposure and flashing, or fogging. Ordinarily, these are things we wish to avoid, but under controlled conditions we can neatly turn them to our advantage.

Aside from strictly practical reasons, it is interesting to use the techniques just to see what you can do with them. Furthermore, they will lead you to many insights on how photography works.

● Things You Need

We will again use the list on page 65, since there is no point in being repetitious. To it you might add the following:

A 1-gallon juice container (optional)
An immersion heater, the size used in coffee cups (optional)
A clamp-on light fixture with a 7½-watt frosted bulb
Light dimmer or rheostat (optional)
Small graduate or measuring cup
Surgical cotton

Juice container: It should be deep enough so that you can put a curled 8×10 print in it vertically and have it covered all the way with water. If you wish, you can use a tray instead, though it is not quite as convenient.

Heater: If you have no running hot water in your darkroom you will find it handy. Otherwise, you will be making frequent trips to the kitchen for hot water. In a moment you will see that hot water is very good to have on hand for purposes other than print contrast reduction.

Dimmer: for easily controlling the intensity of light falling on a print during flashing exposures. However, you can also control it by moving the light source farther away.

Measuring cup: A pint-size one used for cooking is all right. For finer measurements use one of the plastic containers that Kodak 35-mm film cassettes come in; it holds exactly one ounce.

• Developer Dilution: the Basic Method

You have already read that underdeveloping a print will reduce its contrast but that the image may come out mottled if you go too far. Therefore, underdevelopment (usually combined with overexposure) should be carefully avoided. But not always. If you can circumvent the mottle, which is easily done, you can safely underdevelop as much as you wish, thereby flattening prints up to four or five contrast grades. However, the results are usually more handsome if you settle for just one or two grades.

The basic method is to expose a test strip, soak it in warm water (100 F) for two minutes, then put it in diluted developer for two minutes. You can use any dilution you like, but 1:20 is a good starting place for a considerable reduction in contrast. The figure 1:20 is a "dilution ratio." The first number in such a ratio is always the chemical to be diluted (Dektol stock solution); the number after the colon always indicates the amount of solvent (water) to be added. In this instance, you can also express it as one part of Dektol to twenty of water, or just Dektol 1:20. Similarly, one could have a dilution of three to one (3:1) or one to fifty (1:50).

As usual with a developed test strip, the best tone tells you your exposure. In this case it will represent what one would ordinarily consider overexposure, but it will look quite normal on the strip and be the correct exposure for a finished print presoaked in warm water and developed in Dektol 1:20.

• Mottle

A print that has been underdeveloped in normally diluted Dektol (1:2) often has a disagreeable mottle, because different parts of the emulsion absorb the developer at different rates. Thus some areas will be almost fully developed and others half developed, which gives us mottle. One reason for this is that small areas of the gelatin emulsion may vary in toughness, thus varying in absorbency, too. Another is that a print developer diluted 1:2 works very rapidly and erratically. A third is uneven agitation. In a normal print these things don't matter so much, because nearly all the exposed silver halide particles are going to get reduced to metallic silver, anyway. The tones even themselves out.

Unfortunately, this is not true with prints that are deliberately overexposed and underdeveloped: a large percentage of the exposed silver halide crystals are not converted to metallic silver but remain undeveloped. This is what makes the contrast-reduction technique work. However, the uneven absorbency of the gelatin, inadequate agitation and high developer activity must be counteracted, or we will get mottle. We must therefore do three things: soften the gelatin, dilute the developer, and use a high-efficiency agitation technique.

• Warm-Water Presoak

We can help matters considerably by softening the emulsion somewhat with a two-minute presoak in warm water just before development. Then the developer can enter the gelatin at a uniform rate in all areas, provided that the agitation is adequate.

The temperature should be about 100 F. If it falls much lower than that the gelatin won't get soft enough. If it goes over 110 degrees, you may get little black specks and marks.

On some resin-coated (RC) papers the emulsions aren't tough enough and are poorly bonded to their white plastic bases, so it isn't safe to soften them. They may get sticky and even slide right off. However, Kodak RC papers are entirely safe to work with, yet they should be handled with care. Though they are very vulnerable to scratches before processing they are quite tough when wet. Nearly all regular papers can take warm water with no trouble.

● Hot-Water Burning-In

While we are on the subject of warm water, we will take a short detour, then get back to our main theme. Heat can be used to "force" parts of a print that have received an exposure that is not quite enough to permit them to develop. They are on the verge of being developable but actually won't make it. We usually see this in prints that are a little light on one side or in certain areas.

To darken a side, fill the juice container with water at about 125 F. Then curl the print and dip the light side in for about a second, repeating the treatment once or twice if necessary. If it is still too light, return the print to the developer tray for ten seconds to get the emulsion filled with developer again, then dip it another time or two. If you push the treatment any farther than this you may get fog, but not always.

To darken smaller areas, rub them gently with a wad of cotton that has been dipped in hot water and partly squeezed out (so the water won't dribble). Both tricks work best on prints that have developed 1½ minutes or more, and they will work only if the light areas are on the verge of being developable.

For a print that is *over*exposed on one side and normally exposed on the other, use a different trick. When the first side has developed far enough, slide it into the stop bath, leaving the other side sticking out so that it can continue to develop. If necessary, you can keep putting fresh developer on it with your fingertips.

End of detour.

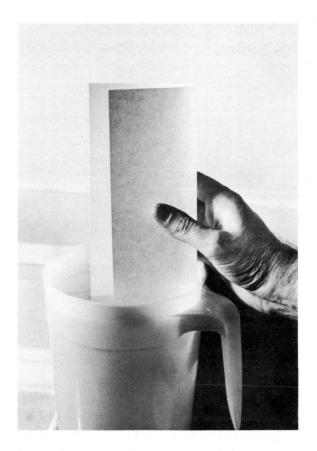

Prints to be developed in a dilute developer should be given a presoak in hot water, which can conveniently be kept in a large juice container.

● Agitation Technique

Print agitation is simple and easy if almost all of the exposed silver halide is supposed to get developed, which is usually the case. However, in developer dilution prints, the areas with *little* exposure will develop most of the way, whereas those with *heavy* exposure will remain mostly undeveloped, which is a kind of pardox. Nevertheless, the latter areas will remain so heavily prone to development that a poor developer flow pattern due to faulty agitation may result in their uneven development. For example, an area that

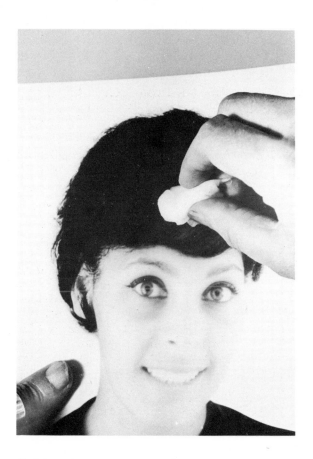

Slightly underexposed areas of a print can be darkened with hot water in a cotton swab.

• Exposure, Contrast, and Developer Dilutions

The useful range of developer dilutions is quite long. For experimenting with the technique, you might try the following: 1:5–1:10–1:15–1:20–1:50–1:100. With lower dilutions and a warm-water presoak, little or no increase in exposure is necessary, but with higher ones you may run into very long exposures—up to two or three minutes or more.

For a lower dilution, make a test strip with a series of five-second exposure times, but increase the individual exposures up to twenty or thirty seconds each for high dilutions.

As you increase the exposure and dilute the developer you get progressively less contrast, until you reach a point where there is hardly any at all. One usually goes this far only for pictorial reasons or just to see what the results will look like. If you merely wish to drop your paper one or two contrast grades, work with the 1:5 or 1:10 dilution.

• Developing Times

With all dilutions, it is probably best to use a two-minute developing time after a two-minute presoak. However, if you find that a print hasn't had enough exposure to develop up in that time you can safely increase it to five minutes or more if the developer is quite dilute. This will bring up the image, but it will also give you more contrast than you would get in only two minutes. To hold the contrast low, you should make another print, giving it more exposure.

However, you may want this extra contrast. For example, you may be using a 1:10 dilution and discover that it drops the contrast a bit more than you desire. By cutting the print exposure and extending the developing time, you can bring it back to where it should be. Indeed, if you develop long enough you can get the same contrast from a 1:10 dilution as you would get from a 1:2.

should have a flat, even tone may come out with streaks.

The ideal developer flow pattern on a print is totally random, that is, entirely erratic and unpredictable. A good way to establish such a pattern is to drag a soggy piece of cotton around the print surface during the entire developing time. Do your best to never make the same movement twice and to cover all parts of the picture about the same number of times. Make the cotton move around like an inebriated toad with a broken compass: erratically. This will give you an impeccable flow pattern and very even print tones.

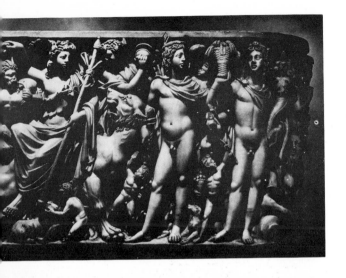

A series of prints made on no. 5 (high-contrast) paper and processed in developers at various dilutions. The idea is to show you how much contrast can be reduced with this method. The progressive dilutions were 1:2 (normal), 1:10, 1:20, 1:30, and 1:40. This gives us a contrast range much greater than one can get with graded-contrast or variable-contrast papers developed at a normal dilution.

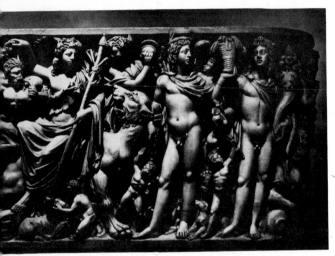

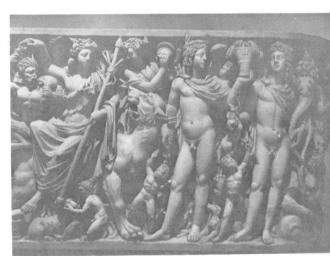

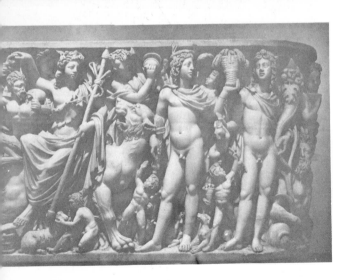

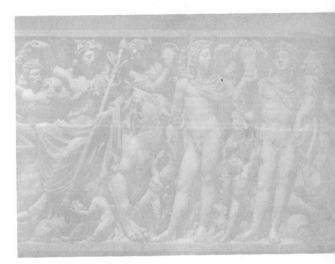

Overexposure and a diluted developer can be used to produce a print that will cut back very fast in potassium ferricyanide bleach. Since the contrast will be reduced, start with a paper two contrast grades too high. A, B, and C were all printed on a no. 5 paper, but A was developed in Dektol 1:2, while the dilution for B and C was 1:20. This made it easy and fast to cut out the background on C. Print C also has the desired amount of contrast.

A

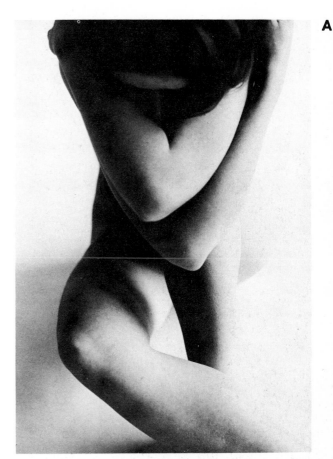

B

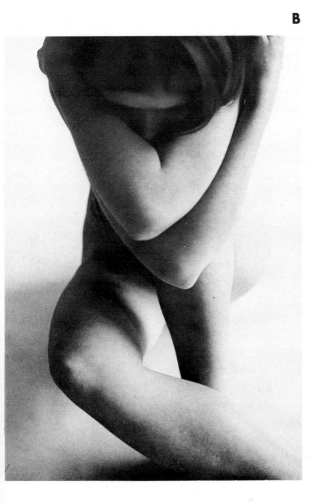

C

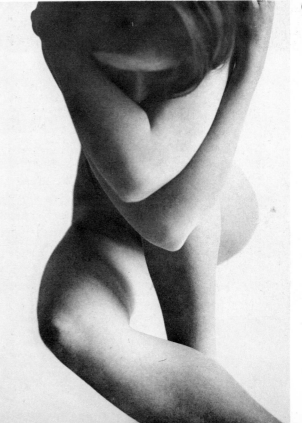

● Developer Exhaustion

Since there may be little developer in it a dilution may not hold up very long. You can probably develop half a dozen 8×10 prints in a tray of 1:20 before it weakens very much, but when you go as high as 1:50 or 1:100 it might be best to mix a new dilution after each print or two.

At the very high dilutions, the developer will get exhausted without even being used. In ten or fifteen minutes the oxygen in the air and that dissolved in the water will oxydize, or exhaust, the small amount of developing agent.

● Print Toning

Most papers change color considerably when they are processed in developers of progressively greater dilution, the particular colors that you get depending on the brand of paper you are using. A given paper may range from a slightly warmish color at 1:5 to a beautiful red-brown at, say, 1:30. The only way you can tell what colors you will get with a paper is to try it, but you can count on their being handsome. In truth, developer dilution prints often look as if they had been treated in special print "toners."

● Bleaching

When you wish to bleach areas in a print down to white, it may take quite a while, especially if the areas are fairly dark. You can speed up the bleaching action by using a developer dilution print. Try a 1:20 dilution as a starting point. Since the contrast will drop, compensate in advance by using a paper or printing filter two or three grades higher than you normally would use for the negative. The print contrast will shift neatly into place and the bleaching will be easier.

● Contrast Control by Flashing

You can reduce the contrast of a print by deliberately fogging it, but that also makes it too dark. However, if you use an underexposed print it can come out with both the right contrast and the desired tone. Actually, you expose a print twice, giving it the basic exposure with the enlarger light and a fogging (flashing) exposure with a white light. Naturally, the two exposures have to be quantitatively related in the right way, or the print won't look right. This is no problem, because we can use a special kind of test strip to determine both exposures at once.

The flashing technique will permit you to reduce contrast very dramatically; for example, you can drop an Agfa Brovira no. 6 (the highest-contrast paper available) down to a minus 4 or 5 and perhaps lower. You would seldom want to go that far, but you can if you wish.

Unlike developer dilution, there is no color change from contrast reduction by flashing, no matter how far you push it. Furthermore, there is no need to presoak the paper or use the special agitation technique just described. Ordinary procedures are quite adequate. This is not to say you should get sloppy; just use the techniques described on pages 33–35.

● Light Source for Flashing

For flashing we need a low-wattage light source, because the print is given relatively little exposure. A small bulb at the right distance from the print will permit us to use flashing exposure times that are long enough to be marked off with a metronome or an electronic exposure timer, or by counting seconds.

Fortunately, the right size and type of light source is available, a small round frosted 7½-watt bulb that will fit standard light sockets. Before using it, tape a three-inch cylinder of black paper around it, so that it won't scatter too much light around the darkroom. Then position it exactly five feet above the surface on which you will flash your prints. With most printing papers, you will then get flashing exposures that are long enough to be manageable.

However, some papers are "faster" (more sensitive to light) than others. If you should find yourself using a type too fast for the setup just described, move the light farther away or tape a few thicknesses of typing paper over the black paper

A light source for contrast reduction by flashing. It is also used for solarizing. It has a 7½-watt white bulb and a short snoot of black paper.

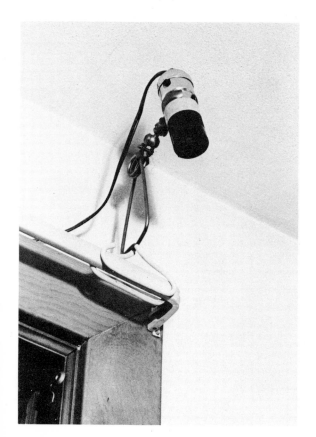

snoot. If you like, you can use a light dimmer, so that you can move the light a lot closer. Or you could use a 25-watt frosted red bulb as your light source. Red bulbs that large are no longer "safe" for papers; they have about the same effect on them as very low-wattage white bulbs.

● The Method in Brief

Make an ordinary test strip on a one-inch strip of paper, then a two-way strip on a full sheet of it. From the latter, select the combination of exposures that will give you both the over-all tone and the contrast you want for your print. Expose your print first with the enlarger, next with the flashing light. Process it in the normal way.

● The Two-Way Test Strip

The reason for making a preliminary test strip is that we only want underexposures on our two-way test, so we have to get the data for exposing it. That is, we make a small strip to get the exposures for a larger one. We don't want *over*exposed areas on the full-sheet test, because they would all be wasted. For the initial strip use the 5–5–5 method (page 56).

After processing it, calculate what you should do to make a full-sheet strip in which the darkest area would be either a normal exposure or slightly under. You might have to change the aperture, the exposure times, or both. If you are a little uncertain of what you are doing, check your exposure figures by making another one-inch strip. Don't be alarmed because some of the areas have no tone in them at all; they're supposed to be that way for this particular technique.

117

Now use the enlarger setting and times you have decided on and use your enlarger to make a test strip on a full sheet of paper. Next, position the paper under the flashing light and use it to expose another test strip right on top of the first one. This time, however, move the cardboard at right angles to the first strip so you will get a checkerboard effect.

For both series of exposures, you should expose by progressively covering up the paper. However, the first exposure of the basic exposure series should be made with a narrow width of the paper covered. Do this also with the flashing series. This will give you a vertical column of basic exposures that have no flashing. You can use them for comparison to the rest to see what flashing actually does. You will also have one horizontal row of flashing exposures with no basic exposures, also for comparison purposes.

For your two-way test strip, four flashing exposures of three seconds each will probably be enough—if you use the recommended lighting setup and Brovira no. 6 paper. This will give you a five-step flashing scale from zero to twelve seconds. With other papers, this flashing exposure range may be either too long or too short. If it is long, cut the exposure times or move the bulb farther away. If it's short, increase the times or the number of steps. Or you could move the flashing light closer.

After exposure, process the two-way strip normally. Remember that you should *never* jerk a test strip or develop it too long. Even the world's most badly exposed strip has useful information on it, but only if you develop it exactly as you intend to develop your finished print.

Find the area that you like best for your final print, then count up to it from the bottom for the first exposure time, in to it from the side for the second. If your two-way strip doesn't look anything like the illustration in this chapter, figure out what is wrong and make another. It will take a whole sheet of paper, true enough, but it will save you money in the long run by simply helping you to see what you are doing.

● The Range of Usable Underexposures

How much you should underexpose with the enlarger depends on how much you want the contrast lessened: the less the first exposure the lower the contrast. The useful range is from nearly normal exposure to about three stops under. If you follow the directions in the last section you will see these data visually laid out for you in the form of a two-way test strip and won't have to bother to figure out such things as the meaning of "three stops." Indeed, test strips are especially for people who aren't good at figures.

From your two-way test strips you can see that as first exposures (enlarger) decrease, second exposures (flashing light) should increase, and vice versa. Again, instead of having to figure it out mathematically, all you have to do is look and see.

A two-way full-page test strip for determining enlarger-light and flashing-light exposures for a method of reducing picture contrast by flashing. First you make a test strip with the enlarger and the negative. Then you use the flashing light to make another test strip right on top of the first one but crosswise to it. To determine the two exposures for a given area, count up from the bottom by fives (0–5–10–15–20–etc.) for the enlarger exposure, then count in from the left by threes (0–3–6–9–etc.) for the flashing exposure. Following this procedure, we see that area Z on the test strip received a ten-second enlarger exposure and a six-second flashing exposure. In vertical column X there are only enlarger exposures; thus it is just like a regular one-inch test strip. In horizontal row Y there are only flashing exposures; therefore, it shows how long it takes to fog unexposed paper with the flashing light. We can see the fog clearly in the 12-second area on the bottom row. Although it is also in the two areas right above it it doesn't look too bad. Comparing them to the two areas to the left of them we can see there has been an improvement. Note that in column X the five- and ten-second areas have no image in them at all. As we move over to the right we can see where flashing has brought the hidden image out.

total
exposure
times
with the
enlarger

Column X

40
seconds

35

30

25

20

15

10

5

0

Row Y

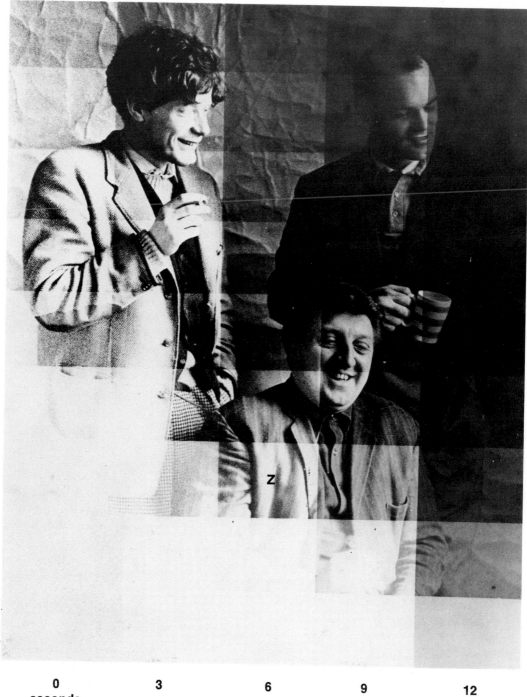

Z

0
seconds

3

6

9

12

total exposure times with the flashing light

A

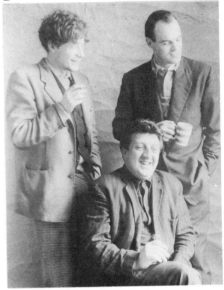

| enlarger exposures | 5 seconds |
| flashing exposures | 9 seconds |

B

10

7½

E

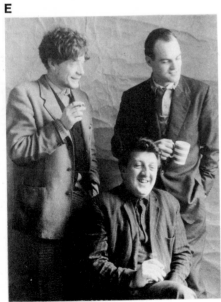

| enlarger exposures | 25 seconds |
| flashing exposures | 4½ seconds |

F

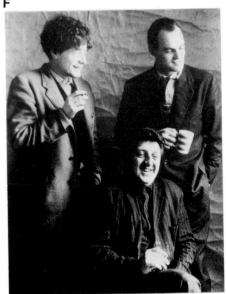

35

3

C

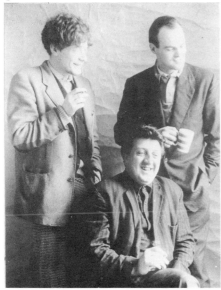

15

7

D

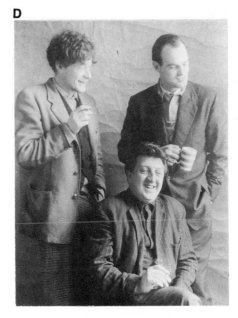

20

6

G

45

0

A series of prints made on Brovira no. 6, as was the two-way test strip. The range of contrasts you see here is considerably greater than you could get with graded-contrast or variable-contrast papers. In working with contrast reduction this extreme, the fogging exposure sometimes makes a print look gray and dismal. This can be corrected by over-all bleaching. We see that print A is quite a bit flatter than one would usually want, though such low contrast can sometimes have decorative possibilities. Print G, with no flashing at all, is quite a bit too contrasty. Print E seems about right; it is two or three contrast grades flatter than G.

• Preflashing

So far we have talked about postflashing, that is, doing it after the basic exposure. You can also do the flashing first, even days ahead, and use the very same flashing times. Thus you can use the same two-way test strip for both methods. Make one for every type and contrast grade of paper you intend to flash.

If you should inherit a truckload of no. 5 or 6 paper it would be good to preflash a lot of it down to grades 4, 3, 2, 1 and possibly 0 (you need it now and then). Or you might find an army-surplus buy or a hot deal on high-contrast papers in 500-sheet quantities. On the other hand, you might try preflashing just to test your wings and see if you have learned anything from this book.

• Effective Paper Speed

In the developer dilution method, you in essence reduce the speed of a paper to practically nil; remember the long exposure times at high dilutions? With the flashing technique, we can increase it considerably, whether we postflash, preflash, or flash during development (yes). You can increase the speed of film the same way, deriving the necessary data with two-way test strips. You see, the things you are learning here can be used in more ways than you supposed.

If you don't really believe that paper speed is increased a lot by flashing, look at your full-sheet test strips. How about those areas with no image at all that develop very substantial images as the amount of flashing exposure is increased?

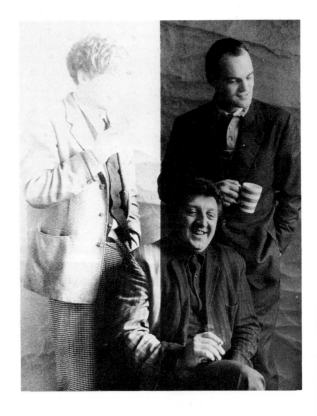

It is hard to tell the dramatic effect of flashing from looking at a test strip or at prints arranged in a series of gradually changing contrast. This print shows rather positively how much difference flashing can make. The whole print was exposed with the enlarger and negative, but only half of it was flashed. You can figure out approximately what the two exposures must have been by analyzing the two-way test strip, which was made on the same brand and contrast grade of paper.

HOW TO SOLARIZE YOUR PRINTS

In the preceding chapter, you were told that prints for contrast reduction can be flashed before the basic exposure, after it, or during development. The latter method is a little tricky, because your prints may get all or partly "solarized." However, you may want them that way, which is another matter. Solarizations are often very interesting, and the phenomenon itself is fascinating.

If a normal or underexposed print is given a brief flashing exposure about halfway through development, it will soon turn gray or black and look thoroughly "fogged." With even less exposure to white light it may merely lose contrast and not look fogged at all. As we move toward *longer* exposures, however, there is a point where some very weird things begin to happen.

By now, you know that the more exposure you give a print the darker it will be. This is a way of stating the Law of Reciprocity, upon which photography is based. But there are times when the law fails to work, for example in solarization. With exposure increases (by flashing) given during development, the print tones may come out progressively lighter instead of darker. At the same time, certain light tones may get dramatically darker. And there may be strange linear effects: along the edges between light and dark areas we may get strong, thin lines that are either light or dark. It is not known why these things happen, but we do know how to control them.

You have seen that flashing is a technique for contrast reduction. It reduces it in solarization printing too, which is not what we want this time. So we have to compensate in advance by using a contrasty negative and a printing paper of the highest possible contrast, which happens to be Agfa's Brovira no. 6. We can also compensate later by bleaching, either local or over-all. Usually, we need to use all three methods on the same picture. It is easier to hold the contrast when we make solarizations from color slides, because they are more contrasty than negatives to begin with.

Unless you carefully control basic exposure, first development, flashing exposure, and second development, your results will prove unpredictable and unsatisfactory. One problem is to slow down both the first and the second development times, which we do by using a 1:10 developer dilution. Another is to find a dim enough light source to give us second exposures that are long enough to control. For this purpose, we use the flashing setup described in the previous chapter, except that we flash the print in a tray filled with water.

If you carefully follow the instructions, you will find that successful solarization is really quite easy. You will surely be astonished by the variety of strange results you can get from just one negative.

● Things You Need

Materials and equipment for printing (list on page 65)
Materials and equipment for print bleaching (pages 90–92)
A lighting setup for flashing (pages 110–11)
An extra tray

A preliminary test strip made on Brovira no. 6 and developed two minutes in Dektol diluted 1:10. Exposure increments of ten seconds were used. The objective was to find a lens aperture setting that would give us a "normal" exposure near the top of the strip and progressively underexposed areas below it.

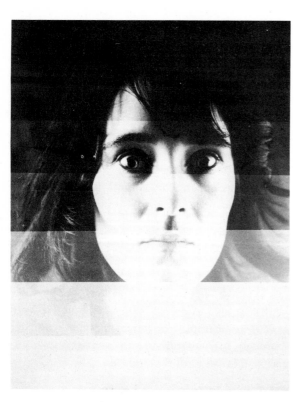

Brovira no. 6 paper
A rather contrasty negative
A color slide

● Step by Step Print Solarization

1. Fill a tray with Dektol diluted 1:10. Arrange the stop bath, first hypo, second hypo, and water holding bath in the usual way.

2. Fill the extra tray with water and position it directly under the flashing light.

3. With the enlarger and a cardboard, expose a preliminary one-inch test strip, using the 5–5–5 method. After fixation, analyze the strip and decide what aperture setting would be best for a two-way test strip. Or you may wish to change the exposure times.

4. With a whole sheet of paper, make the enlarger exposures for a two-way test strip, using the figures you have just worked out. Develop the printing paper for two minutes in Dektol 1:10.

5. Then put it in the tray of water beneath the flashing light source, agitating it for about fifteen seconds, then letting it sit there for another forty-five. Push the print to the bottom of the tray and make sure there are no air bubbles in the water.

6. Holding the piece of cardboard at right angles to the first test strip exposures, use the flashing light to make a second set of exposures. Use the exposures 3–3–3 seconds, etc. For the first exposure, cover about one inch of the paper to give yourself a column of reference tones with no flashing exposures.

7. Put the two-way strip back into the 1:10 Dektol and develop it for an additional two minutes. Process it normally the rest of the way.

8. Analyze the test strip. If it doesn't look approximately like the illustration of the two-way solarized test strip in this chapter, figure out what went wrong and make another. Remember that by remaking test strips you will save time and money in the long run.

9. If the two-way test strip is satisfactory, find the portions that look promising and use their exposure times for making finished prints.

• Don't Jerk It!

Any time that a print seems to be getting much too dark during the second development, let it go the full two minutes anyway. You can cut it back later with bleach. If you jerk it too soon you may have a problem with mottle.

On the other hand, if a print doesn't come up enough in the two minutes, you can safely extend the time even up to five or ten minutes. At ten minutes you may get fog or developer stain but, again, you may not. It is worth the risk. Since the picture will look a little peculiar anyway, a little fog shouldn't hurt it.

• The Useful Range for Flashing Exposures

With Brovira no. 6 and the prescribed flashing setup, the workable range for flashing exposures should be from about three to fifteen seconds, which is about the same as the range for contrast reduction by flashing (preceding chapter).

If you prefer to use a rheostat or a 25-watt red bulb, night light, Christmas-tree light, or some other light source, you will have to determine for yourself the best exposures by making one or more two-way test strips.

The above range for flashing exposures will work on high-contrast papers other than Brovira no. 6, for example on Kodabrome RC Ultra Hard (no. 5). However, other papers won't give quite as much contrast.

• Data from Other People

It would be nice if you could directly use data from photography books and magazines, but it sometimes doesn't work out very well. There are always certain differences between your equipment and materials and those used by authors in developing their figures. Thus their data will seldom apply exactly to your situation. However, you can safely use them as a starting point for your own experiments. In this book the most important thing is method; with it, you can derive accurate figures for yourself.

• Agitation for Over-all Bleaching

Solarized prints usually react well to bleach, and the methods given on pages 90–101 will work very well on them. Since you now know about "impeccable" agitation (preceding chapter), we will add it to the lore on bleaching. When you agitate by tray tipping or pushing the print around, the bleach moves over the edges of the print at a higher speed than over the rest of it. This causes the edges to bleach too fast, especially if the tones are light. If you use the randomized-toad method with a cotton swab it will even out the bleaching very nicely.

• Color Effects

The color effects that we encounter in using the higher developer dilutions can also be brought into solarization. The trick is to use Dektol 1:10 for the first development and a higher dilution, say 1:30 or 1:40, for the second, but with the same developing times. If necessary you can extend them, but don't cut them. You can also add color by using a 100 F water prebath before the first development. With either approach or both used together, you will need revised first and second exposure times. Determine them with preliminary and two-way test strips.

total
enlarger
exposures

35
seconds

30

25

20

15

10

5

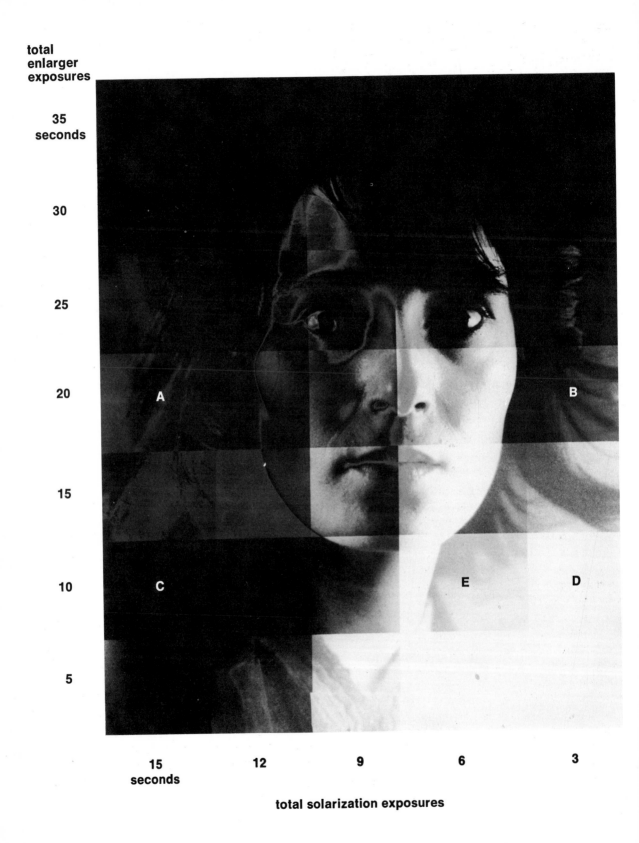

15
seconds

12

9

6

3

total solarization exposures

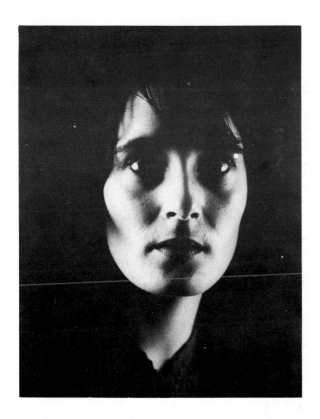

This is a normal, or reference, print made on Brovira no. 6, which is much too contrasty for this particular negative if one wishes to treat it as an ordinary portrait. It was exposed normally for this particular contrast grade and developed normally for 1½ minutes in Dektol 1:2. Having such a reference print will help you keep track of what the solarization process is doing to the image contrast.

A two-way solarization test strip made on Brovira no. 6. Such a high contrast of paper was used to compensate for an anticipated loss of contrast in the solarization process. The first series of exposures was made with the negative and the enlarger light. Then the paper was developed in Dektol diluted 1:10 for two minutes. Next it was put in a tray of clean water for a minute, after which it was given a series of solarization (flashing) exposures. Immediately afterward, it was developed another two minutes in the diluted Dektol, then run through the stop bath and fixer.

Note that areas A and B are almost exactly alike in tone, though A got a 15-second flashing exposure and B only three seconds. C, with the same solarization exposure as A and ten seconds *less* enlarger exposure still came out much darker than A, which is difficult to explain, though scientists are still trying. Though A and B, with the same enlarger exposure, are tonally alike, C and D, each with ten seconds' enlarger exposure, are greatly different in tone. This is also hard to explain. Area E shows a result similar to what one would get with the flashing procedure explained in the preceding chapter.

● Use Color Slides

You can make black-and-white pictures from color slides, which usually come out as "print negatives." That is, their light and dark tones are reversed. Some subjects look very good as negatives. You can also make solarizations from color slides, using the exposure-determination methods just described. You will probably discover only one real difference: some slides—mainly those with a preponderance of yellow, brown, orange, or red—will require considerably longer first exposures than negatives do, but that is an easy problem. Second exposures will be the same, as will the processing times.

In order to get sharp pictures, you must remove color transparencies from their slide mounts. Information on preparing individual frames for enlargement will be given in the next chapter.

127

A series of prints in which the ratio of enlarger exposure to solarization exposure has been varied considerably. All were made on Brovira no. 6 to compensate for loss of contrast. Note how very different the images are from each other, and how strange some of the effects are. Print E, however, merely looks as if it had been printed on a no. 0 paper and has no peculiarities of tone and line.

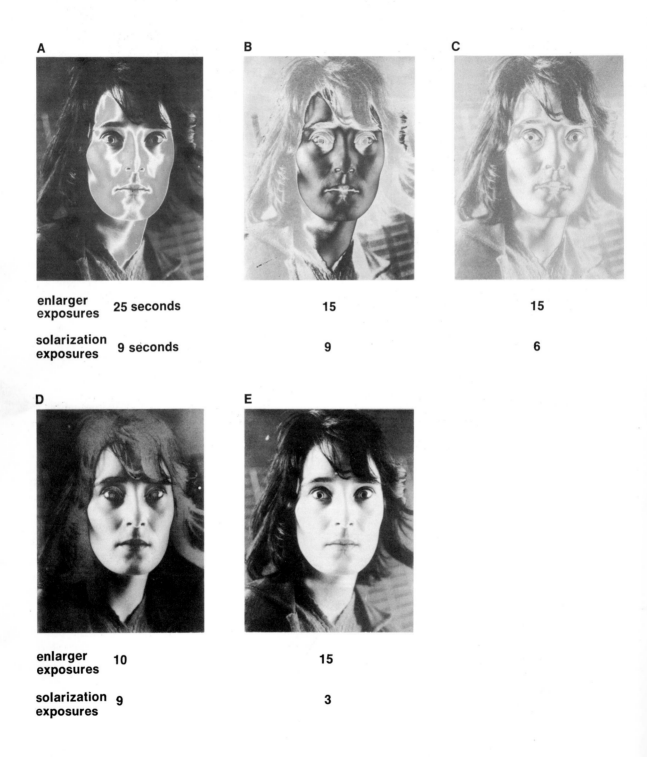

A

B

C

| enlarger exposures | 25 seconds | 15 | 15 |
| solarization exposures | 9 seconds | 9 | 6 |

D

E

| enlarger exposures | 10 | 15 |
| solarization exposures | 9 | 3 |

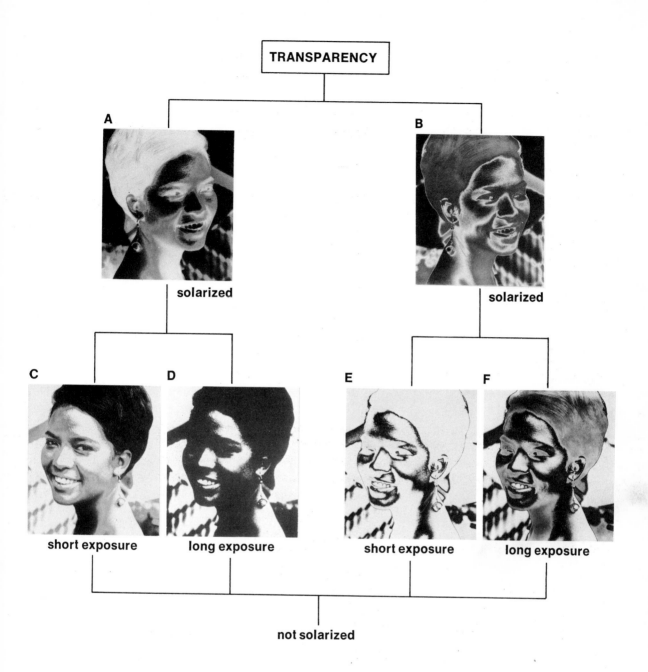

TRANSPARENCY

A
solarized

B
solarized

C
short exposure

D
long exposure

E
short exposure

F
long exposure

not solarized

A series of pictures printed on no. 5 resin-coated (RC) paper. They originate from a color slide, not a negative. A and B were made directly from the slide. Then A was used as a paper negative (next chapter) to make C and D; and E and F were contact-printed from B. A two-way solarization test strip was made to get the enlarger and solarization exposures for A and B. C, D, E, and F are straight contact prints without solarization exposures. However, you can easily solarize contact prints if you wish, after two minutes' development in Dektol 1:10.

HOW TO MAKE BLACK-AND-WHITE PRINTS FROM COLOR SLIDES   HOW TO COPY PRINTS

Can you make black-and-white pictures from color slides? Yes, you can easily make prints of the very highest quality. The method is very simple: you merely put a slide in your enlarger and make a print from it, which comes out as a "paper negative." After it has been processed and dried, you use it to make a contact print on an unexposed piece of printing paper. You go through exactly the same steps in making such a print as you would in contacting film negatives (pages 31–33). There is really nothing to it.

You can do this with any kind of enlarging paper, but there is grain in the paper base of an ordinary paper that will show up in the final positive print. In some pictures it looks very good, yet we would rather do without it most of the time. Furthermore, it takes quite a bit of fiddling around to make a paper-grain print look right, mainly because it looks like a mezzotint or lithograph. These art forms aren't too well adapted to most photographic subjects.

Fortunately, resin-coated (RC) papers are virtually grainless, because their emulsions are coated on white plasticized paper that is very thin. Thus if you use an RC paper for your paper negative you will get hardly any grain at all, except that originating in the slide itself. Now, if you should use a slide made with one of the

Kodachromes for your paper negative, it would produce a print with much finer grain than you ordinarily get by printing film negatives. Color films other than the Kodachrome type usually have quite a bit more of it, though it is seldom excessive.

If you have color negatives, you can make high-quality prints directly, without having to make intermediate paper negatives. Just handle them as if they were ordinary black-and-white negatives. They usually require longer exposure times, but that is about all.

● Things You Need

Printing materials and tools
Bleaching materials and tools
Retouching materials and tools
Kodabrome RC paper, Soft or Medium (no. 1 or no. 2)
or Polycontrast Rapid RC and printing filters
The tape-laminated glass plate used for making contacts
A sponge-rubber typewriter or area-rug pad
Ready-Mounts for color slides
Color slides
Color negatives
Scissors

Black paper
Ruler
Scotch tape

Most of these things have already been explained sufficiently. For 8×10 prints, the typewriter pad should be cut down to about 10×12 inches. It is to put under the unexposed paper, the paper negative, and the glass when you are making an exposure for a contact print. It helps hold the paper and the negative in tight contact, thus assuring sharpness in the final print. The other new tools and materials will be explained as we go along.

• The Contrast of Color Slides (Transparencies)

Color slides are generally quite a bit more contrasty than black-and-white negatives, though it doesn't seem as if they are. This means that you have to deliberately hold down the contrast when you are making a paper negative and again when you are making a print from it. Though you can use the contrast-reducing techniques from pages 110–22, it would be simpler if you could get along without them.

Fortunately, most slides will make fine black-and-white pictures if you make both the paper negatives and the final prints on a no. 2 (medium) RC paper or use a no. 2 printing filter with Polycontrast Rapid RC. However, some of the prints will tend to be a little on the "brilliant" side, that is, just a bit too contrasty.

We can easily get around the problem by making our negatives on no. 1 paper (soft) or using a no. 1 printing filter. If some of them should turn out to be a little too soft we can easily bring up the contrast again by printing them on a harder paper, for example a no. 3 (hard) or no. 4 (extra hard). You see, there is no rule that we have to make our paper negatives and final prints on the same grade of paper.

In this technique we need an RC paper only for making the "paper" negative, because that gets us around the paper-grain problem. Once

you have the paper negative you can print it on any kind of paper you wish with good results, because the grain problem enters in only at the negative stage.

On rare occasions you will have a color slide that is too contrasty for even a no. 1 paper negative and a no. 1 final print. In that case, remake the negative on no. 1 and reduce the contrast even more by using a 1:10 or 1:20 developer dilution, or use the flashing technique. Sometimes you may wish to use these techniques for strictly pictorial purposes or just to see what you can do with them. Since color transparencies will record a remarkable range of tones, you may merely want to know how much detail you can bring out in both the dark and highlight areas of your prints.

• Step by Step in Making a Black-and-White Print from a Color Slide

1. Remove the slide from its mount and prepare it for enlargement.

2. Clean it carefully, just as you would a negative.

3. Expose a one-inch test strip on Kodabrome RC Soft (no. 1) paper or Polycontrast Rapid RC with a no. 1 filter. Process it normally.

4. Using the exposure data obtained from the strip, expose a full sheet of the same paper and process it normally. You now have a paper negative.

5. Remove the transparency from the enlarger and open up the lens two or three stops; you need more light because it will have to go through the white base of the paper negative in order to expose the final print. Acting only as a light source, the enlarger doesn't need to be stopped down for sharpness.

6. Center the sponge-rubber pad on the enlarger baseboard directly under the lens. To make sure that the rectangle of light will cover it you may have to raise the enlarger head a few inches.

7. Make a one-inch test strip from the paper negative; put a strip of unexposed paper emulsion

up in the center of the pad and cover it with the paper negative, emulsion (image side) down. Cover both with the glass plate. Expose and process the test strip normally. If necessary, make another one.

8. Examine the test strip to decide on the exposure and the contrast of paper (or printing filter) for the final print.

9. Expose and process the final print.

• Preparing the Transparency

Color transparencies curl a little bit in their cardboard mounts. Slide projectors compensate for this but enlargers do not. Consequently, if you make a paper negative with a mounted slide it will be out of focus either in the center or around the edges. Thus it must be removed from the mount so that the negative carrier and the weight of the enlarger head will flatten it properly.

Since single frames are difficult to clean and to position in negative carriers, you should Scotch-tape narrow strips of thin black paper to two opposite ends of each transparency. They will give you something to hold onto. The black paper that comes in packages of printing paper is about the right thickness. The strips should be of the same width as the film.

After you are through printing, you will have some unmounted color transparencies, which can't be projected. Easy enough. Buy some "Ready-Mounts" from the photo store and remount them yourself. There is nothing to it.

• Clean the Glass

To prevent extra dust spots on your paper negative and final print, you should carefully clean the tape-laminated glass plate (glass sandwich). Use a lintless cloth or paper towel and detergent or ordinary soap and water. Then dust it off frequently while you are using it.

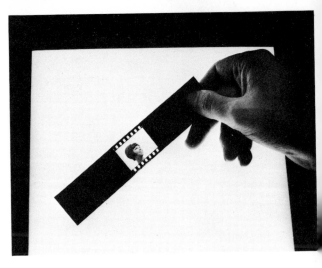

Held in front of a light box, this transparency has been removed from its slide mount and prepared for conversion into black-and-white prints. The ends are black paper taped on with Scotch tape.

• Judging Paper-Negative Quality

People who make paper negatives usually underexpose them quite a bit without being aware of it. The reason is clear enough, once you have had it explained to you. The first problem is that superficial appearances may be deceptive. For example, a paper negative that looks exactly as a perfect film negative should is actually underexposed approximately one stop (50 per cent). This doesn't seem to make sense.

What happens is that judgment is misled by the fact that we gauge the quality of a film negative by the light coming through it from behind (transmitted light), whereas we gauge a paper negative by the light falling upon it (reflected light). Though it is natural to do it this way, it just doesn't work in the case of the paper negative.

What really counts, however, is what a negative of either kind does to *transmitted* light. Therefore one should judge a paper negative by holding it up to a fairly strong (150-watt) tungsten light source or to a bright section of the sky. Viewed this way, a paper negative that looks up to one stop (100 per cent) overexposed when examined by reflected light will look (and be) just right. You have to get used to the fact that it looks too heavy by room light.

Underexposed paper negatives that look normal by room light will often make good prints, but they tend to lack brilliance and detail in the shadows. On the other hand, paper negatives that look much too heavy (dark, dense), even by transmitted light, will usually make rather good prints. With overexposed film negatives, we have a grain and sharpness problem; remember? But paper has no discernible grain, no matter how much one overexposes it. In contact printing, we burn right through any fuzziness due to heavy density, making it sharp again. This is not to encourage sloppiness in figuring out exposures but to get you over your fear of paper negatives that look too dark in room light.

A paper negative positioned partly in front of a light box, so that part of it is seen by transmitted light, the remainder by reflected light. The sections seen by reflected light seem too overexposed (dark, dense) for a good negative. However, all negatives should be judged by transmitted light. The light box shows that this paper negative has been exposed correctly, for it looks very good by transmitted light.

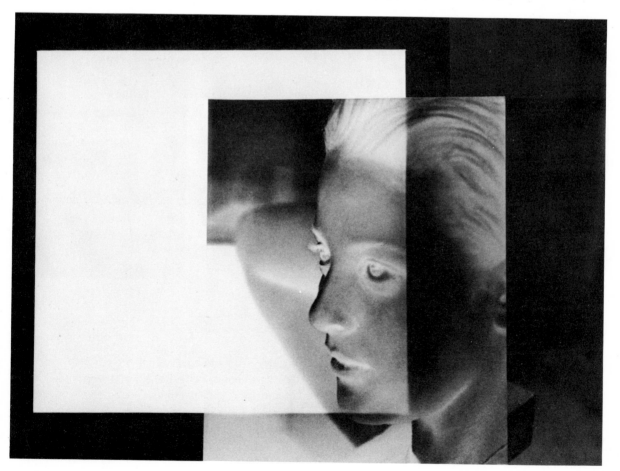

2 stops underexposed　　　　**1 stop underexposed**　　　　**normal negative**

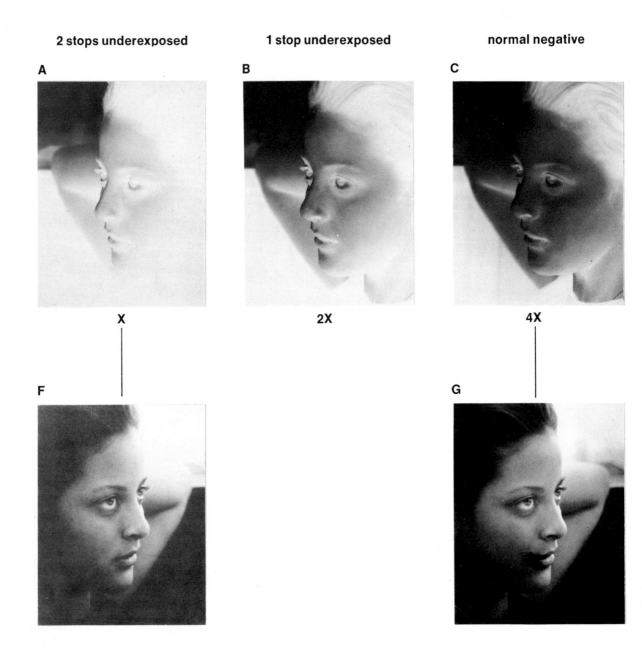

A series of paper negatives that are one stop apart in exposure. That is, starting at the left the exposures were progressively doubled. This set shows you how paper negatives look by reflected light—ordinary bright room light. Negative A is badly underexposed and hardly usable. B is also under (one stop). Though it looks too dark in room light, C is the normal negative. Though D

1 stop overexposed　　　　**2 stops overexposed**

D　　　　　　　　　　　　　　**E**

8X　　　　　　　　　　　　**16X**　　　　**EXPOSURE (X)**

H

and E are overexposed, they will·make good prints. However, the contact-printing exposure for E, heavily overexposed, is very long. The contact print from A (print F) is washed out, muddy, and weak. However, the print from E (print H) is hard to distinguish from the one made from negative C (print G).

• Dodging and Burning-In

You should make your first paper negative and final print without any dodging, burning-in, bleaching, or retouching. If you try doing everything at once, you will get all mixed up. In fact you will probably get thoroughly confused by the next four paragraphs.

The easiest time to do either dodging or burning-in is when you are making the paper negative from the color slide, because you can see the image projected by the enlarger onto the printing paper. However, in making the final print you see nothing but bright light shining on the white back of the paper negative, which is contact-printed, emulsion to emulsion with the unexposed paper. Things like burning-in corners and dodging the center are easy enough to do at the final print stage, but you can't even see the smaller areas that you would like to burn-in or dodge. Thus you have to estimate their position or not attempt to work on them.

On page 72 you learned that the basic exposure time limits the number of areas you can substantially dodge in a print, but that you can burn-in as much as you please. For reasons that will sound peculiar, you are not thus limited when working from color transparencies. You see, burning-in the paper negative accomplishes the same thing as dodging the final print, so you can get a myriad of areas in the final print that are lightened as much as you desire. You get them by simply burning-in the paper negative. Figure it out.

At the same time, dodging the paper negative does the same thing as burning-in the final print. To make areas come out darker on the final print, you can dodge them on the paper negative, but the amount of dodging you can do is limited by the basic exposure time. Thus only a limited number of areas in the final print can be darkened in this manner. However, when you are making the final print itself you can darken as many areas as you like, because you now do it by burning-in.

In making prints directly from negatives, you can do an infinite amount of local darkening but only a limited amount of lightening. In making them from positive transparencies, you can do an infinite amount of both. This is confusing, of course. By the time you have it figured out, you will have considerably increased your understanding of "negative-positive processes" and your insights on what actually makes photography work.

• Which Side Is Which? Up or Down?

When we print directly from a black-and-white film negative, we position it emulsion (dull side) down in the enlarger, but a color slide should be positioned emulsion up. The image then comes out reversed from left to right in the paper negative. The final print reverses it back to its normal position.

With many color films, there is no dull side to use as a guide, but the words and numbers printed along the edges will work just as well. If they read backwards when you hold a positive transparency up to the light, it means that the emulsion side is toward you.

Use a different method for locating the emulsion of a Kodacolor-X negative. There are little arrows or pointers along one edge. When you hold the film so that the arrows are along the top edge and pointing to the right, the emulsion side is toward you.

When you make black-and-white prints from Kodacolor negatives, you don't make paper negatives. You should therefore position them emulsion down in the enlarger.

• Dye Retouching and Bleaching

All that you have learned about dye retouching and bleaching can be applied when you are making black-and-white prints from either positive or negative color transparencies. When you are working from a color positive (color slide), you also get a sizable negative to work on, which you haven't had before.

One of the easiest and most exciting things to do is to make areas come out white in the final print. You can do this by bleaching the print, of course, but it can be a tedious job if the areas are fairly dark. It is much faster and easier to just paint them out on the emulsion side of the paper negative with Kodak black opaque. Since no light will go through the opaque, they print up pristine white. Mistakes with the opaque can easily be removed with a wad of damp cotton, so you can work over an area as many times as necessary.

You can also get white lines by drawing on the paper negative with a well-pointed china marker (use a razor blade) or a nylon-tip pen. If you are careful, you can do good shading with a china marker, and you can rub off your mistakes with a dry cloth or cotton and lighter fluid. If you don't want the texture of your shading to show, do it on the back of the paper negative.

You can bleach things on the paper negative to make them come out darker in the final print; and you can put dye on them to make them come out lighter. At the paper-negative stage, the ultimate effects of bleaching and dyeing are reversed, just as are the effects of dodging and burning-in. After you have worked on the paper negative, you still have the final print to play with, if you like. An additional bonus is that mistakes in dyeing and bleaching can often be patched up on the finished print.

• Prints from Color Negatives

You have already been told enough about making black-and-white prints from color negatives to permit you to go ahead on your own. All you need to know is that they should be put into the enlarger emulsion down and that they require a

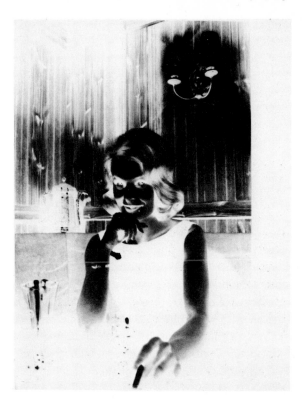

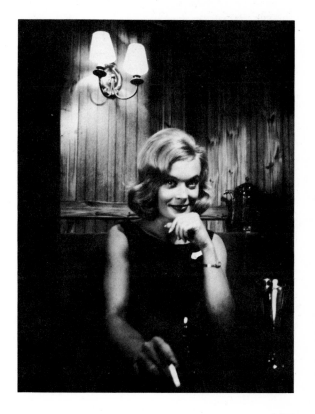

A paper negative and print from a very contrasty color transparency.

longer exposure than do black-and-white negatives.

Even so, some extra information might be helpful. The best choice for a color negative film to use would be one of the Kodacolors. The requirement for a longer exposure in black-and-white printing comes from the fact that a Kodacolor negative is orange in color. This is because it has a dye-masking layer, which we needn't explain here. The orange color is all you need to know about.

Now, black-and white printing papers are deliberately made so that they are relatively insensitive to red, yellow, yellow-green, and orange light. This is so that we can work with them under safelights of the same colors. Thus when you put a Kodacolor negative into the enlarger you are in essence putting a safelight filter in with it. With a long enough exposure, however, you overcome the effect of the orange filter layer and end up with a print of good quality.

Since you know the exposure times will be longer, you should increase the individual times in your test strips. For example, instead of using five-second exposures, you could go to ten or fifteen seconds.

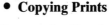

• Copying Prints

In most families there are pictures that uncles and aunts want copies of, but they seldom get them, because the negatives are missing and the family photographer (you) doesn't know how to make copies. Let us solve this nagging problem.

The first thing you need is lighting that is very even, intense, and diffuse. The best source of it is skylight on a clear sunny day, so tape up your pictures on the shady side of the house or garage. Line them all up at eye level, then go down the line taking pictures with a hand-held camera. If you can't get up close enough with your camera, buy a supplementary close-up lens for it (you will find many other uses for it).

A paper negative and print from a transparency with a tremendous amount of fine detail in it. We see how the negative looks by reflected light: much too dark. However, by transmitted light (on a light box) it looks good. It preserves all the details in the shadows and darker mid tones.

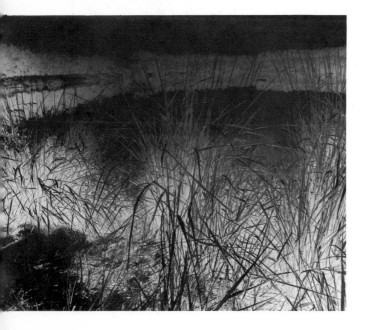

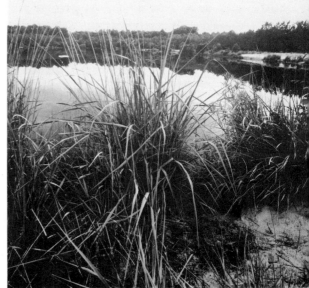

Be sure to get your camera properly squared away to each picture so that their opposite edges are parallel in the viewfinder. If you don't consciously keep track of the edges they nearly always come out skewed. Otherwise not.

Determine your exposure by reading a Kodak gray card held flat against one of the pictures. For a built-in meter, bring the camera close enough to fill the whole viewfinder with the gray card. If you have a separate meter, hold it about five inches away. If you have no meter at all, refer to the data sheet that comes with the film and use the recommendation for "open sky." Shoot at f/4 or f/5.6.

In order to get both slides and prints of all the pictures, you should use one of the Kodachromes. When you take your exposed film to the drugstore, ask them to have Kodak process it (not someone else) and send it back unmounted. Then use the paper-negative process you have just been reading about. Kodachrome contrast and fine grain are just right for it.

After you have made your first paper negative and final print, you can set up an assembly line and really rip along. Do it by using the same paper-negative and final-print exposures for all the rest of the copy transparencies.

They will be a handsome bluish color, incidentally—much prettier for projection than strictly black-and-white pictures. When you are finished printing, you can put them in Ready-Mounts.

One nice thing about having a paper negative is that you can make all the prints you wish from it. It is much less prone to scratches than a film negative. And you can dodge, burn-in, bleach, dye, and crop it.

If you don't wish to take the time to make paper negatives and are not interested in slides, make your copies on a Kodacolor. Then you can make black-and-white prints directly. Both the contrast and grain are good, though they are even better with a Kodachrome.

One reason for using skylight is that it is very bright on a sunny day, so that you can photograph at a shutter speed high enough to compen-

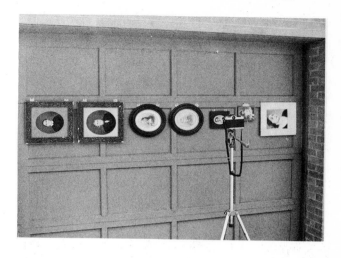

Family pictures aligned on a garage door for quick copying. If you have a steady camera hand you won't need a tripod.

sate for your quivering and shaking. Even so, you should make a deliberate effort to steady yourself and your camera. Slow down your breathing, brace the camera by jamming it tightly against your forehead, and grip it so that your index finger has no function whatever in holding onto it. This finger should be so free and independent that you can use it to slowly *squeeze* on the shutter release without jarring the fingers that are actually holding the camera.

However, if you are a really flipped character with a high-speed quiver you will have to take additional measures. You can use a tripod with a cable release to steady your camera. Or you can tape your pictures to the sunny side of the house and use a considerably higher shutter speed for hand-holding your camera. If you opt to do the latter, work at a time of day—morning or afternoon—when the sun will fall upon the pictures at an angle of about 45 degrees.

Sunlight is both bright and even, of course, but it is not diffuse. Skylight, which is highly diffused, tends to fill in or hide scratches and other blemishes on the surfaces of pictures. But direct sunlight sets them out in high relief. If your pictures are unmarred, however, you can use it all you like.

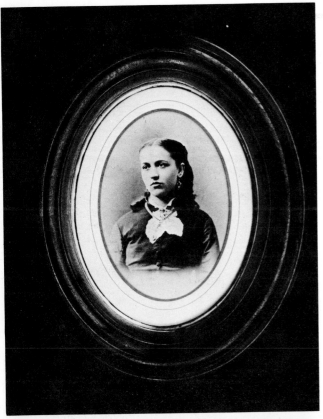

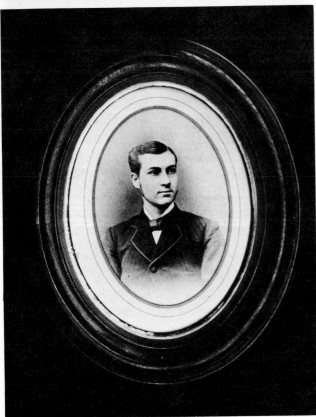

Color slides made in sunlight from black-and-white pictures won't come out so blue, but they will probably have a color cast of some hue—from little defects in manufacture or processing. Fortunately, slides look good with a bit of color.

● Ghostly Fuzzigrams

You can make rather interesting fuzzy, or diffuse, pictures in several ways. If you chose the right transparencies to make them from, they can look very good, either as negatives or positives. However, fuzziness is something we ordinarily attempt to avoid.

One method is to expose the paper negative through the back of the printing paper. That is, instead of positioning the paper emulsion up, which is the usual thing, you turn it face down. The colored image projected by the enlarger falls on the white plastic base, which diffuses it considerably before it gets through to the emulsion on the other side.

Because the plastic base prevents a lot of the enlarger light from getting through it at all, you will have to give a lot of exposure. Use longer exposure times for your test strips, say twenty or thirty seconds.

You can also get your fuzziness through contact printing by positioning a sharp paper-negative emulsion up on the printing paper; and this doesn't require any more exposure than you would generally use in making a final contact print. For even greater diffusion, position the paper negative and the unexposed paper back to back. For this you will need extra exposure, so make a test strip.

Fuzzy prints of normal contrast often look rather muddy. You can usually improve them by making them much more contrasty or very flat and light.

Family pictures that were copied on Kodachrome-X, then converted into paper negatives and contact prints.

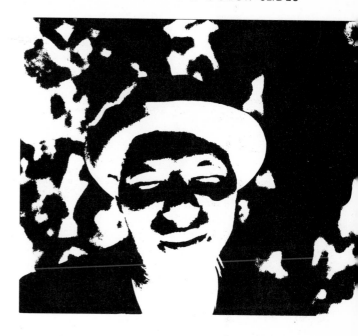

• High-Contrast Prints

One of photography's favorite sports is to convert images with an ordinary range of light, medium, and dark tones into pictures with only black and white in them. They are very dramatic and often look like wood or linoleum block prints. The trick is to work from transparencies that already have a lot of contrast and print them on high-contrast papers.

Earlier, you learned that color slides generally have a lot of contrast, though not always. We were initially concerned with holding the contrast down, but we are now faced with the problem of building it up even more. As we've seen, it is best to start with a contrasty slide. In a moment you will see that you can also use ones with only moderate contrast, though the method used with them is a bit more involved.

We must define a contrasty color transparency a little better. It is one that has both very light and very dark tones in it. It may also have a whole range of middle tones, and, again, it may not. In either case, we should call the transparency contrasty. High contrast merely means that there is a considerable tonal difference between some areas in a picture. The fact that widely contrasting light and dark tones may have mid tones between them doesn't lessen the contrast, though it seems to. In this technique we get rid of the mid tones, anyway.

With a contrasty color slide, it is dead easy to make a dramatic, high-contrast print. All you do is to make both the paper negative and the final print on Kodabrome RC Ultra Hard (no. 5) paper. Or you might try Ilford Ilfospeed no. 5. The middle tones (grays) ordinarily "drop out," so that only black and white are left. Their absence increases the feeling of contrast. If a few of the grays refuse to drop out, make your final print on Brovira no. 6. One rarely has to go farther than this when working from a contrasty transparency.

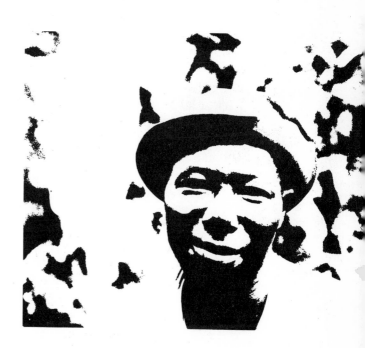

The high-contrast negative was made by printing a rather contrasty transparency on a no. 5 resin-coated (RC) paper. The high-contrast contact print was also made on a no. 5 paper. However, a no. 1 or 2 would have worked just as well, because there are no mid tones in the paper negative.

Since you are not familiar with high-contrast images or with making tones drop out, you should make an abundance of test strips as you go along. After making some preliminary one-inch strips, you might try a slightly different kind of two-way test. Make a full-sheet paper-negative test strip, process and dry it, then put it on a full sheet of unexposed paper and cover both with the glass plate.

Remove the negative from the enlarger, open up two or three stops, and make a second set of test exposures at right angles to the first set. As usual with two-way test strips, you will end up with a checkerboard effect and a lot of useful exposure information.

When you have made your full-sheet paper negative, it may need a bit of cleaning up with bleach and opaque, though not necessarily so. If there are some light tones that haven't quite dropped out, you can usually get rid of them easily by overall bleaching (pages 93–94). On the other hand, they may drop out automatically when you make your final print, so don't be too hasty to start bleaching.

In the white areas of the paper negative (which will print black in the finished print; remember?) there may be some black spots and lines that you wish to get rid of. They would print up as white garbage in the black areas of your final print. Eliminate them with ultra-strong bleach, but take great care not to let it get away from you.

If there are unsightly white things in the black areas of the paper negative, they will print up as black garbage in the final print. Fill them in with black opaque. Except when you are working along the contours of white areas, you can literally slosh it on, because its black surroundings are going to print up white, anyway. You can also be much freer with bleach than usual, because all the white areas around it will print up black.

Of course, you can use bleach on the final print, though it is seldom necessary. Don't use opaque, because it will show up strongly; use spotting dye instead.

When you work from transparencies of strong contrast (long tonal range), you can almost always get brilliant and clean high-contrast final prints with the above method, often without having to use bleach or opaque. When you use color slides of low or moderate contrast, you may have to add two additional steps; they are as easy as candy, so don't worry about them.

To get the extra contrast that is needed, all you do is make a contact print from the final print, as if it were a paper negative. This will give you another negative (called a "second-generation negative"). In making it you increase the contrast even more and drop out additional tones.

Then you contact-print the second-generation negative and get a second-generation positive, again increasing contrast and dropping out mid tones. You may call this positive a "final-final print," if you like. It might help you keep your head sorted out—or it might not.

Go through all the steps, the standard ones and the extras, with Kodabrome RC Ultra Hard. However, you can shift to Brovira no. 6 for the final-final print if you need more contrast and still have tones to drop, which is unlikely.

Since people seem to have a great thirst for pictorial contrast, you will probably find this whole business fascinating. And it will certainly teach you a lot about positive-negative processes in photography.

• Conclusion

You have come to the end of this book on laboratory techniques for the beginner. It is full of simple and workable recipes. Though the techniques were designed especially for you they are also good enough for any professional. Thus you will never have to abandon them in favor of something better.

The accent throughout has been on method, for with method you can figure out almost anything for yourself. So as you stumble along through life, remember the humble test strip with love and reverence; it is the golden key to the Law of Reciprocity, upon which all of photography is based, and the very essence of photographic method.

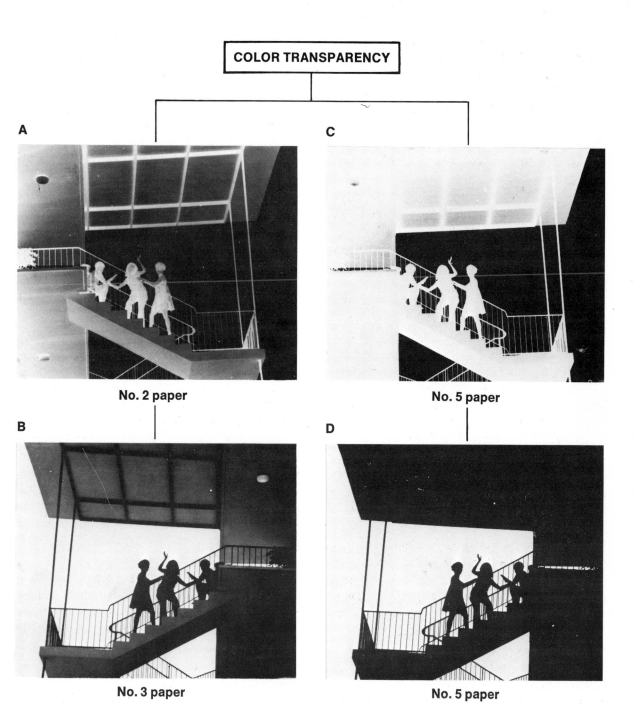

COLOR TRANSPARENCY

A

No. 2 paper

B

No. 3 paper

C

No. 5 paper

D

No. 5 paper

Frequently, you can make both a normal black-and-white print and a high-contrast one from the same color slide. You create the difference by your choice of paper contrast grades. Note that mid-tone detail disappears when no. 5 paper is used. This is called "dropping out" tones.

APPENDIX

• Photographic Papers

To learn what various photographic papers look like, go to a photo store and ask to see their paper sample books. While there, buy the inexpensive booklet *Kodak Photographic Papers (G-1)*.

Contact and enlargement types: Contact papers are made only for use with contact printers, which have very bright light sources. Enlarging papers are for use with enlargers, which have relatively dim light sources; however, they can also be used for contact printing (pages 31–35, 132–42). Do not use regular contact paper for enlargements of any kind.

Paper speed: Contact papers are extremely slow (insensitive to light), which is why they shouldn't be exposed with an enlarger light source. Though they are much faster than contact papers, the different types of enlarging papers vary considerably in speed, from slow enlarging papers to fast ones.

With fast papers such as Kodabromide or Polycontrast Rapid you should make sure that your darkroom is properly light-trapped (pages 11–13) and that your safelight is actually safe. Otherwise you will get fog. There is less of a problem with slow papers, but they do require longer exposure times.

With a given type of paper, the lower contrast grades are considerably faster than the higher ones. A variable-contrast paper, such as Polycontrast Rapid, is fastest when no filter is used. A no. 1 filter cuts the speed about 30 per cent, and it drops quickly as progressively higher filters are used. To help you keep track of speed and exposure differences, there is a little enlarging computer bound into Kodak's *Darkroom Dataguide,* which is also recommended as a basic workbook.

Image tone: The so-called black-and-white papers may actually deviate quite a bit from neutral-black image tones. Contact papers are usually bluish black. The color scale for Kodak enlarging papers (recommended for quality and availability) runs from neutral-black (Kodabromide, Kodabrome RC, Polycontrast Rapid RC) to warm-black (Polycontrast, Polycontrast Rapid, Medalist, Panalure), and finally to brown-black (Opal, Ektalure, Polylure).

The tonal warmth of warm-black and brown-black papers can be varied considerably by using special developing techniques and special developers. With both paper types, Dektol produces comparatively cold tones that can be made even colder by extending the developing time. A short developing time in Dektol, or higher-than-normal developer dilutions (pages 110–16), will make them warmer. For results going even further toward brown or red-brown, one should develop warm-black and brown-black papers in Selectol, Selectol Soft, or D-52, which are usually described as "portrait developers." The brown-black papers (Opal, Ektalure, Polylure) are affected most by them.

The most popular papers are the neutral-black ones, because they will go well with many kinds of pictures. Warmer papers are used mainly for portraits and romantic landscapes.

Tint: If an emulsion is coated on a tinted-paper base, the base color will show in the image. Kodak's main paper-base colors are white, cream white, and old ivory (buff). All are handsome, but white is by far the most popular.

Weight: Photographic papers come in different thicknesses, or weights, which are usually designated by capital letters: SW (single weight), MW (medium weight), and DW (double weight). Resin-coated (RC) papers are medium weight, while regular papers are usually available in both single and double weights. Though they cost less than the others, it is best to avoid single-weight papers, because they are harder to handle, easily damaged, and produce prints that tend to curl badly and look generally scruffy.

Bases: Emulsions are usually coated on either paper or plastic bases, though materials such as glass, cloth, and metal may also be used. There is now a strong trend toward white resin-coated paper bases for photographic papers, mainly because processing, washing, and drying times are thereby considerably shortened.

Surfaces: When an emulsion is being coated on either a resin layer or paper a texture can be embossed on it. This texture, or small pattern, is called its "surface." Kodak paper surfaces are designated by the capital letters A, B, D, E, F, G, J, K, N, R, V, X, Y, and Z. Examine a sample book to see what they look like, because we will describe just a few of them here.

Surface A: A smooth, lustrous surface on a white lightweight stock (base). Because it can easily be folded without cracking the emulsion, it is often used for letters and French-fold greeting cards.

Surface F: A surface that can be given a glossy, mirror-like sheen by "ferrotyping" (drying a print face down on a chromium-plated metal sheet). Drying a print in open air or between blotters produces a high luster. This is photography's most popular surface, for both amateurs and professionals. RC papers with the F surface will come out glossy without being ferrotyped.

Surface N: A very smooth, fine matte surface that will take pencil, ink, dye, and opaque very well and is thus exceptionally good where extensive retouching is required. Since it is available in Kodak resin-coated (RC) papers, one should use it for paper negatives that require subtle retouching, which can most easily be done with chalk or pencil dust (pages 153–54).

Surface Y: Simulating silk, this is a very bright and attractive texture.

Surface Z: Simulates canvas. This surface in Opal Z paper is frequently oil-colored with opaque oils, thus creating the effect of an oil painting on canvas.

Contrast compensation: If you print the same negative on both a glossy and a matte or semi-matte paper you will see that the glossy print seems to have quite a bit more contrast. Thus a print that looks just right on a no. 2 F surface will look one or two contrast grades too flat on a no. 2 N or Z surface. There are two easy ways around this problem: buy a higher-contrast grade of paper than you usually do, or extend your negative-developing time by 50 per cent to make your negatives more contrasty.

● Print Toners

After they have been thoroughly washed, prints can be toned various colors (mostly hues of brown) in special "toners," some of them available in concentrated-liquid form, others in the powder form. In most cases, a print is put into a tray of toner, at room temperature or warmed somewhat, until the desired color arrives. However, with certain sepia toners the print is first bleached, then redeveloped in a toner. It is very easy to do.

Though most toners yield red-brown, purple-brown, and chocolate hues, there are also red, blue, and green toners available. Of the latter group, only the Kodak blue toner is worth bothering with. Kodak doesn't make red and green toners, but other companies do. Don't try them unless you like lurid colors.

Good print washing is usually very critical, so use a Perma Wash bath (pages 34–35), even with resin-coated (RC) papers, and at least quadruple the times for both the first and second washes. Use a fast flow of water and agitate the prints constantly by pulling them up from the bottom and putting them on top. The actual toning instructions—very simple—come with the bottles or packages of toner.

Since the emulsions of various kinds of paper differ chemically from one another they do not react in the same way to a given toner. Therefore, toners and papers must be paired properly (with a wrong pairing there is usually no reaction at all). In the Kodak *Darkroom Dataguide* the recommended combinations for Kodak papers are listed. They are also given with the information that comes in each package of printing paper. For example, for Kodabrome RC paper we find the following Kodak toners recommended: blue, brown, sepia, sulfide sepia T-7a, and polysulfide T-8, all of them excellent toners.

There is no way for you to learn exactly what effect you will get with a given toner until you try it for yourself, because examples of what it can do are often not available. However, you will be safe enough if you start out with Kodak toners sold in packets or as liquid concentrates.

• Summer Storage of Films and Papers

In hot and humid weather, film and paper will begin to deteriorate, especially if the packages have been opened. To prevent this, use them as soon as you can—or bundle them up in plastic food wrap and store them in the refrigerator. Stored this way, they will stay in good condition for about two years. If you wish them to last considerably longer than this, put your film and paper in the freezer section.

When you remove film from the refrigerator, the moisture in its package or cassette will condense on it, so you have to wait several hours for it to disappear—longer if the film has been frozen; don't use it until then. Unless it has been frozen, however, you can usually use paper right after taking it out of cold storage, but if you feel any moisture on the emulsion, let the paper warm up for a while.

• How to Make Borderless Easels

Easels with masking leaves (for making prints with white borders of various widths) are usually quite expensive; at least the good ones are. If you can get along without the white border, you can make yourself an effective easel for a few cents. Many people actually prefer borderless prints, because they like the way they look. They also get a lot of image size for their money, whereas borders can cut it down considerably.

The simplest easel for, say, 8×10 prints requires only a 2×12-inch strip of light cardboard, eight short lengths of masking tape, and an 8×10 piece of printing paper to focus on. First, put your negative in the enlarger and get the image size, focus, and cropping you want on the focusing paper, moving it into exactly the right position. Next, temporarily anchor the paper to the enlarger baseboard with two pieces of tape. Then butt the cardboard strip up to the ten-inch side of the paper that is farther from you and tape it there with two pieces of tape at right angles to it. Position them so that they and the cardboard strip exactly bracket two corners of the focusing paper.

Now take four pieces of tape and loop them back on themselves, sticky side out, making sticky-tabs for holding down printing paper. Remove the focusing paper and rub down a sticky-tab for each corner. You now have an effective easel. To use it, turn out the white light, fit a piece of enlarging paper into the brackets along the cardboard strip, and press its corners down fairly hard with a clean cloth (not with bare fingers!). Expose the paper and process it.

One problem with this simple easel is that you have to reposition the cardboard strip and sticky-tabs every time you make a new cropping or print another negative. You get used to it, but it does take time. Another thing is that the looped-tape tabs soon get filled with paper particles from regular papers (but not RC) and don't stay sticky very long, though you can renew the stickiness with lighter fluid. Also, they tend to pull off the baseboard when you lift up the paper after exposing it.

You can partly solve the tab problem with car-

A borderless easel constructed right on the enlarger baseboard with a strip of cardboard, two pieces of masking tape, and four masking-tape sticky-tabs.

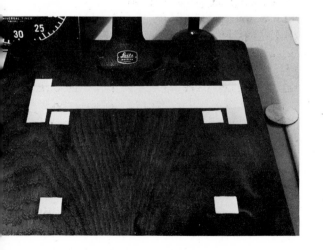

pet tape, but you have to use it carefully, because it is terribly sticky. If you rub your prints down too hard on it they may tear when you try to lift them up. Carpet-tape sticky-tabs get filled with paper particles too, but it takes a lot longer. If you rub them down hard to the baseboard with a spoon handle they won't tend to pull up with the paper, providing that you don't rub the paper down on them too hard.

You can solve the repositioning problem by making your easel mobile instead of stationary. Cover one side of an $11\times14\times\frac{3}{4}$-inch piece of plywood with either white or black Con-Tact paper. If you prefer, you can use $\frac{1}{4}$-inch tempered Masonite, a piece of 1×12 board, or even an empty 100-sheet paper box that has something in it to give it weight. You will have a skidding problem, so turn your easel over and glue about two dozen rubber hose washers to the bottom.

If you use white Con-Tact, you can crop and focus your images without using a focusing paper. However, your pictures will then be out of focus by the thickness of the printing paper, though stopping down will probably take care of this. Even so, it would be better to have a 4×5 piece of paper to do your focusing on. If you use a focus magnifier, you won't need the small focusing paper. Just glue a piece of printing paper to the bottom of it. This will compensate for the focus difference between the white Con-Tact paper and a focusing paper.

After you have covered your board with Con-Tact paper and firmly rubbed it down, you can affix the cardboard strip, tape brackets, and sticky-tabs to the top of it. You will now have a mobile, all-purpose borderless easel with rubber treads.

If you use white Con-Tact paper, incidentally, it will reflect a small amount of light back through the printing paper during exposures, increasing the image contrast somewhat. Black Con-Tact won't do this, but you would find it difficult to tell what difference it makes. The surfaces of commercially made easels are black, white, or yellow, so you can see that color doesn't matter much.

A movable borderless easel made on a piece of chip board covered with Con-Tact paper. The tape borders and sticky-tabs are set for 8×10 paper. For 11×14 paper—or any other size—they would have to be moved, which takes but a moment.

Sticky-tabs made with a single piece of tape will pull up when you remove your paper from the easel. If you make each of them with two pieces of tape this won't happen nearly as often. Start with the pieces crossed, sticky side down, and do as the illustration shows.

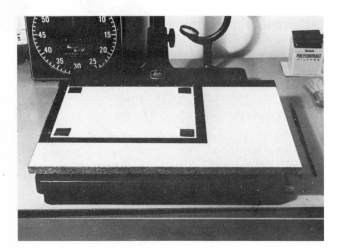

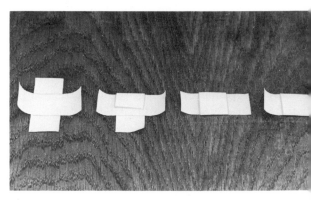

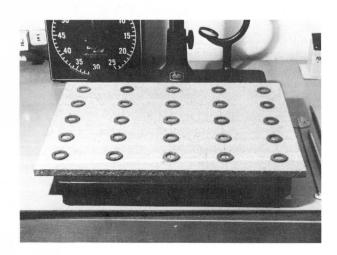

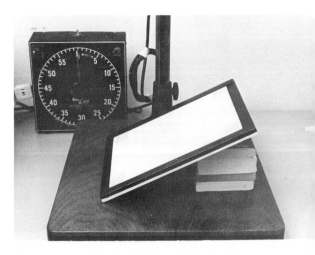

The bottom of an easel, showing rubber hose washers glued on to make a non-skid surface.

By propping one end or side of your easel up with books, you can either correct or create quite a bit of linear distortion in the image.

• How to Correct or Create Distortion

When you aim your camera either upward or downward at a rectangular shape (building, box, wall, etc.) the opposite vertical edges will converge to some degree, depending on the camera angle. This can be disturbing in a picture. However, we can make the edges parallel again by merely tilting the enlarger easel, which we can do by simply propping up one end or side of it with books or boxes. If it tends to slide we can fasten it to the enlarger baseboard with masking tape.

Try this: Put a negative in your enlarger and open the lens all the way for focusing. Put focusing paper on the easel so you can see what you are doing. Now prop up one end of the easel at an angle from twenty to thirty degrees. Position the enlarger head so that the whole frame barely fits on the paper, and focus on the center of the image. Notice that only the center is sharp, the upper and lower parts of the image getting progressively more out of focus.

Now slowly stop down the lens, stop by stop, and observe how the area of sharpness gradually expands both upward and downward. You are demonstrating "depth of field" (or depth of sharpness) to yourself and at the same time preparing to use a tilted easel and still make a picture that is acceptably sharp in all areas. Notice that there is very little depth of field when the aperture is wide open but that stopping down enough will increase it considerably.

With the lens stopped down all the way, your entire image may now be sharp—or it may not quite make it. If not, raise the enlarger head a few inches, open the lens for refocusing, and go through the whole procedure again. Depending on the easel's angle of tilt, the entire image may be sharp at the minimum aperture or even at a somewhat larger opening, because increasing the distance between the lens and the focusing paper also increases the depth of field.

Depending on the height of your enlarger standard, you may be able to raise the head high enough to permit you to get acceptably sharp pictures with the easel tilted from forty-five to seventy degrees. With many pictures, it doesn't really matter if the top and bottom edges are a bit fuzzy or out of focus.

Using a negative that has a distorted rectangular shape in it, tilt the easel just enough to make the skewed lines parallel. Note that the tilt distorts the shape of the image frame so that you have to crop some of it off in order to get a rec-

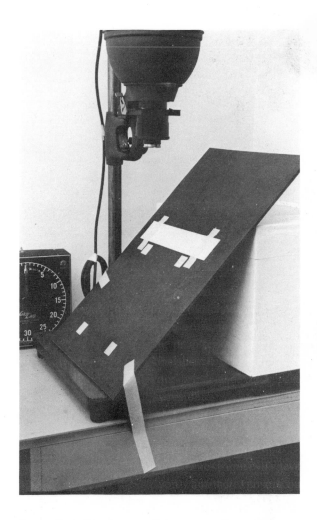

For radical distortion creation or correction, use a piece of cardboard or pressed board propped against a box. Tape it down so that it won't slide. Make a borderless easel on it for positioning and holding the printing paper.

A

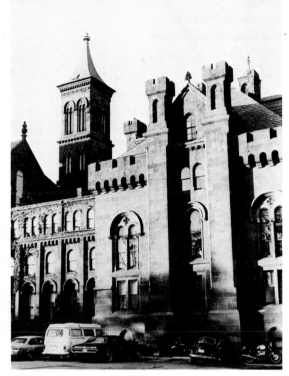

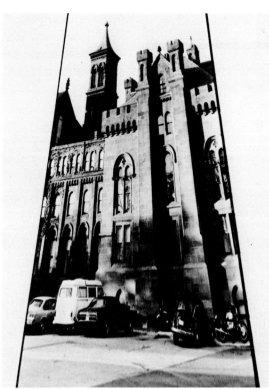

C

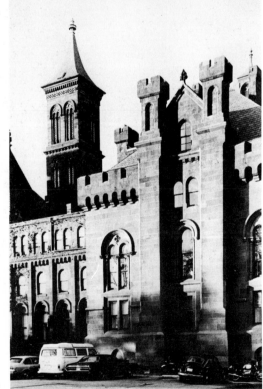

B

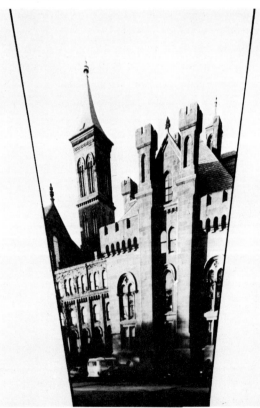

D

tangular picture. Now *increase* the skew of the rectangular thing in the picture, rather than trying to correct it. You may find that increasing distortion, or even introducing it, is more fun than eliminating it.

There is a minor exposure problem. With the easel tilted, the top part of the image is closer to the enlarger light than the bottom part is. Thus the top needs less exposure time. Give the whole print the basic exposure time required by the top, then give the rest of the print additional exposure by burning-in (pages 72–74).

To get the exposure times, make two one-inch test strips, positioning one across the top of the picture for the basic exposure time, the other across the bottom for the burning-in time. Expose them separately but develop them at the same time. Use five-second exposures for the top strip and ten- or fifteen-second ones for the bottom (the greater the angle of easel tilt the longer the exposure times).

The top test strip will give you the basic exposure time for the entire print. To determine the right burning-in time for the bottom of the picture, pick the best exposure in the bottom test strip and subtract the basic exposure time from it. The remainder will be the correct burning-in time. *Figure it out!*

Print A, which is full-frame, is from a negative made with a 50-mm lens. Notice that the vertical parallel lines tend to converge somewhat. In print B, tipping the easel about 20 degrees corrected the convergence. However, some of the image—especially near the top—had to be trimmed off to keep the picture rectangular. Print C shows what happens when we tip the easel in the opposite direction at an angle of about 60 degrees; and print D shows a 60-degree tilt in the previous direction.

You can also use distortion-correction and -creation techniques on subjects other than buildings.

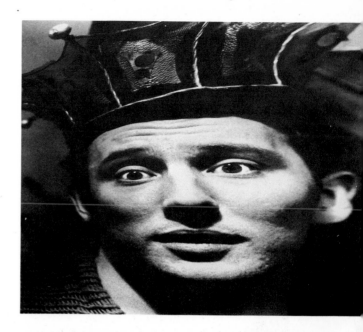

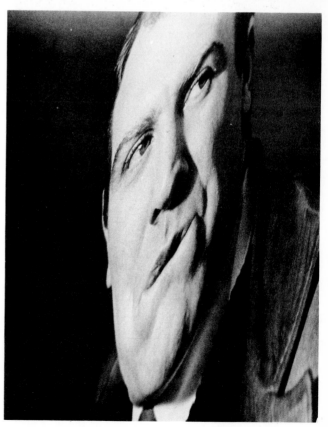

• How to Lighten and Darken Negatives

Sometimes one gets negatives that are either too dark or too light to produce good prints. The dark ones (overexposed and/or overdeveloped) make fuzzy prints with mushy, gray highlights. The light ones (underexposed and/or underdeveloped) make flat prints that are muddy in shadow and mid-tone areas.

Dark (heavy, dense) negatives can be reduced (lightened) with Farmer's reducer, which comes in handy packet form. Buy some packets and carefully follow the easy instructions printed on them. Review the material on print bleaching pages 90–99) because much of it will apply to bleaching negatives. Bleaching, lightening, and reduction mean the same thing.

Light (thin, too-clear) negatives can be intensified (darkened) with chromium intensifier, which also comes in convenient packets. Again, the instructions on the packets are entirely adequate. A given negative can be intensified more than once; the density gradually builds up. This is a three-solution method: bleach, clearing agent, and developer; however, it is very easy to use.

For a one-solution darkener, try Victor's Fine Grain Intensifier (in a handy vial), but don't believe the fine-grain part. Both intensifiers and reducers increase grain in negatives, and you have to learn to live with the fact. However, it is better to have a grainy negative that will print than a less grainy one that won't. As it happens, dense negatives are usually very grainy to start with, though thin ones have finer grain than usual.

With Victor's you can do local intensification, which can be fun, and the intensification can easily be removed just by soaking the negative in hypo.

Negatives that are *very* dark can often be made quite printable with Farmer's reducer, though not always. Remember that this is the same potassium ferricyanide bleach that you use on prints. There are much more restrictive limits on what an *intensifier* will do for a *thin* negative. There has to be at least a little image detail for the intensifier to build on. Where there is none the chemical will do nothing whatever.

• How to Remove Spotting Dye

When you are learning to spot prints, you will probably botch a few jobs, usually by getting dye in the wrong places or using too much of it. Though you should practice on reject prints, you would probably rather not, which means that you will ruin some good pictures. Or will you? Perhaps you can merely remove the dye and start over.

Returning your prints to the hypo bath will remove some of it—if the bath is fresh. However, a fresh bath may also bleach some of the silver if you leave the prints in it long enough for the dye to disappear. And you have to wash and dry them again, which is a drag.

Fortunately, there is a way to safely remove dye from dry prints without having to wash them again. And you can remove just the mistakes and leave the good work untouched. All you need is clear household ammonia, surgical cotton, Q-Tips, and some small pieces of *photographic* blotter.

For bleaching lightly dyed areas, use about twenty drops of ammonia in two ounces of water. Apply the solution gently, because a wet emulsion gets soft and easily damaged. Use a well-loaded Q-Tip or cotton swab and blot the area frequently to take up the dye as the ammonia loosens it from the emulsion.

With heavily dyed areas, you will have to go to stronger ammonia, even using it full strength. This is perfectly all right as long as you work gently and patiently, though it may bleach underdeveloped prints somewhat. If you start rubbing you will dig up the emulsion with the cotton. Unfortunately, you may not be able to get rid of all the dye in very heavily dyed areas, yet you'll be able to lighten them considerably, which is better than nothing.

The active part of an ammonia solution (the ammonia gas itself, NH_3) disappears into the air, as you can tell by the smell. Thus there is no need to wash your prints again after getting rid of the dye. If the smell bothers you, mix the concentrated ammonia with vinegar, fifty-fifty, in two- to four-ounce quantities; then dilute the mixture with water. Warning: don't use ammonia in your spotting brush, for it will dissolve the hairs.

● **How to Color Prints**

Some people love to color photographs with Marshall's transparent oil colors, which are sold in photo stores. They usually color portraits that have been made on matte or semi-matte paper and treated in one of the brown toners. Such papers have a "tooth," so that the color will stick to them instead of rubbing off. The brown tone helps make the Marshall's flesh colors look real, whereas they tend to look rather greenish when applied to untoned black-and-white prints.

There is no trick whatever to using oil colors: you just rub them on and rub them off, cleaning out highlights and trimming up messy edges with a solvent. To make color cover large areas smoothly and easily, there is an oily preparation that you can rub on your prints first. The instructions with the set tell you all you will ever need to know, but most of it has just been recited here.

For more vivid colors that will work on glossy as well as matte and semi-matte surfaces, you can use transparent food and fabric dyes. They will cost you less than oils, but they are quite a bit harder to put on evenly; thus it is best to put them on pictures that have quite a bit of pattern or texture, for this will hide unevenness quite well.

For food colors, which are best because they are brightest, get a Crown Colony or McCormick four-color kit, which will give red, green, blue, and yellow. For a good purple, get gentian violet from the drugstore. Merthiolate will give you a shocking pink. All the other colors you need you can mix with this basic six. For example, Merthiolate with gentian violet will give you an excellent magenta, and green with red makes a fine brown.

Though the colors aren't very chromatic (vibrant), RIT dyes are good (and inexpensive). However, in the liquid form they aren't concentrated enough, so buy the powders. Mix a concentrated solution by dissolving one level half-teaspoonful of powder in one ounce of 70 per cent isopropyl (rubbing) alcohol or in the same amount of water heated to the simmering point. Then strain the resulting concentrate through a fine-weave cloth and put it in a dropper bottle from the drugstore.

The alcohol solution goes on very well, even on glossy prints, but it dries so fast that it is next to impossible to get it on smoothly over large areas. Thus you have to smooth colors out with ammonia (see How to Remove Spotting Dye, above). However, the alcohol mixture is very good for drawing lines and details, and coloring small areas.

The water solution dries more slowly and is thus easier to handle over larger areas (up to a square inch or two), but this is true only if you add five drops of Photo-Flo per ounce to the dye; add a similar amount to the water you rinse your brush in, and use it for diluting the dye concentrate.

You can apply dye with a spotting brush, a Q-Tip, or a cotton ball. You can also put water in a tray, add some dye concentrate, and dip all or part of a presoaked print in it—to get a light, smooth tint. Add five drops of Photo-Flo per ounce to the dilute dye. Remove unwanted dye with ammonia.

● **How to Do Pencil and Chalk Retouching**

If you have tried dye retouching (pages 85–89) you have no doubt found it frustrating, especially if you have worked on glossy-surface prints. Pencil and chalk retouching are much easier to do, but you have to work on matte or semi-matte surfaces. The ideal for this purpose is the Kodak N surface (see Photographic Papers, above).

You can start with a well-sharpened ordinary no. 2 pencil. If you hold it lightly in your hand the lead will go onto the print smoothly. To make the penciling even smoother, rub it with a dry Q-Tip or a small ball of cotton. To clean up the edges of areas, use an artgum eraser that has been cut into a sharp wedge. Use a soft brush to get rid of the eraser crumbs; if you do it with your hand they will leave marks. Or use an artist's kneaded rubber eraser, which leaves no crumbs.

The main shortcomings of this technique are that too much pencil will make a shiny area on your print and that retouched areas can pick up fingerprints. However, a steam treatment will usually solve both problems. If not, you will have to put your print in a picture frame under glass, which will both protect it and minimize the shine.

Steam treatment is most often used for chalked prints (see below). The technique is simple. You merely hold a retouched print face down over a pan of boiling water until the chalked or penciled areas have been thoroughly steamed. Then immediately plunge it into a tray of cold water and lay it out to dry.

The steam softens the emulsion, so that the pencil or chalk particles become embedded in it. Since the gelatin is like a very tough glue, they get stuck so tightly that they won't rub off or shine very much. The cold water merely sets the gelatin before you have a chance to get fingerprints on the chalked or penciled areas. This is an old trick of the so-called salon photographers.

For chalking prints, you need a stick of artist's black chalk, a piece of the finest black sandpaper, dental pumice, surgical cotton, and an artgum eraser. It is also handy to have artist's paper stumps, Q-Tips, and lighter fluid. All these materials are inexpensive.

We start with a little chalk dust, which we make by rubbing the chalk stick on the sandpaper. To the pile, we add an equal amount of pumice and mix them together. If you are working with a toned print, you can add other colors of chalk dust to the mixture to get the right color. The pumice gives the chalk a little "tooth," so that it will bite into the print surface and stick there. Use dental pumice from an old-fashioned drugstore or "technical" pumice from a printers' supply store. Bon Ami is also good, if you can find it.

Rub a ball of cotton, a Q-Tip, or a paper stump into the mixture, then rub it into the print surface with small, circular movements. If the area doesn't get dark enough, apply more of the mixture until it does. If it gets too dark, wipe off the excess with clean cotton. To remove chalk or pencil dust altogether, use cotton and lighter fluid.

Clean up the edges with the wedge-shaped eraser. For "picking out" minute details, you might use lighter fluid and a "mini-Q-Tip," made with a tiny wisp of cotton and a round toothpick. You can also *scratch* out small highlights with a long-pointed X-acto knife or a single-edge razor blade. For merely lightening areas somewhat you might try white chalk dust. White and black can be used on different parts of the same print.

If you wish, you can make pencil dust and use it in the same manner as you would chalk dust. Conte-crayon dust is also very good, and you can get it in black and brown.

For merely filling in dust spots, a no. 2 pencil is too soft and smeary, so get a 3-H and sharpen it to a needle point on fine black sandpaper. The trick is to handle it delicately enough. You should hold it loosely in your hand so it won't dig the print surface, then lift one end of the print off the table while you are penciling. This gives it a little spring. Use the pencil only on areas of light or medium tone, because the shine will show up in dark areas, which should be dye-spotted. Pencil and dye spotting go well together on the same print.

After a picture has been treated, blow off all the chalk or pencil particles (or use a soft brush) and give it the steam-and-cold-water treatment.

• Use a Comparison Patch

Under safelight illumination it is hard to clearly see how your prints are coming along in the developer tray. If you can decide how light the lights are and how dark the darks, it will help you decide when they have developed long enough. Having something to compare the print tones to would be very helpful in the dim light.

For this purpose make a comparison patch by exposing a 4×4-inch piece of photographic paper to the room light and putting it in the developer tray. For judging the dark areas of a print under the safelight, lay the patch across them with the black side up, and use the white side to judge the light areas.

When you are through printing, fix, wash, and dry the patch, so you can use it again.

• How to Demagnetize Your Negatives and Equipment

In the chapter on cleaning negatives, you learned what a headache static electricity can be and were told about anti-static cloths and sprays. Unfortunately, the spray recommended, Marshall's, contains isopropanol and leaves a greasy residue. Like anti-static cloths it is good, but with some shortcomings.

It would be easier to live with isopropanol if we weren't spraying it into the air, as we do with Film Klens. Well, there is an effective anti-static rinse and wetting agent that also appears to contain this chemical but there is no way of spraying it into your own eyes, which should make it considerably safer. This compound is Ecco ✕121, which is made by the Electro-Chemical Products Corporation and is available in photo stores.

The function of this product is to effectively demagnetize (degauss, remove the static charge from) your film during processing in such a manner that it will stay demagnetized as long as possible. For this purpose the degaussing agent was incorporated in a wetting agent that has the same purpose as Photo-Flo. So before you hang your films up to dry, merely substitute Ecco ✕121 for Photo-Flo, using one ounce of the concentrate per gallon of water. When your films have finished washing, soak them for thirty seconds or more in the stuff and hang them right up to dry without wiping them. It works just fine, so good-by static—for a while, at least.

You use this same dilution in a cloth to wipe down negative carriers, film holders, enlargers, easels, work surfaces, and so on. So, you can spray on your isopropanol with Marshall's and wipe it on with Electro-Chemical's. You pays your money and you takes your choice. Happily, both products do a good job, but you should not add them to your menu or use them as a gin substitute in martinis.

• Testing the Stop Bath or Hypo

You should not permit your stop bath to lose its acidity, because it will lead to the ruin, or exhaustion, of the fixing bath in either a one- or a two-bath system. A ruined fixer frequently leads to stains and markings on prints, though they may become evident only after a period of time.

If you use an indicator stop bath it will warn you when it has been used up by turning purplish. However, plain acetic-acid baths have no indicators in them. After they have been in use for a while, such baths should be tested frequently to make sure they haven't conked out.

If you follow the hypo-use schedule given on page 36 you will have no need to test the hypo bath(s). However, you may lose track of how many prints you have run through the system, or you may suspect contamination of some kind, usually from developer carried over from an exhausted stop bath. In such cases the hypo should be tested.

For testing the stop bath and a one- or two-bath fixing system, Kodak makes a little testing outfit accompanied by simple and effective instructions. It takes about a minute to test both a stop bath and a fixer. If you have any doubts about your baths, buy the kit—it should last you for years.

Making a hypo test with the Kodak kit, a simple and fast procedure.

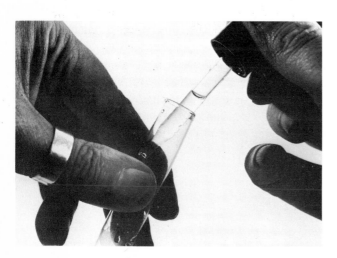

● How to Make Fog Tests

If you are using a non-standard safelight or have a lot of outside light leaking into your darkroom, you ought to run some simple fog tests. You may have a serious fog problem without realizing it, because it may not show up in the white areas and borders of your prints and yet be degrading your images very considerably.

Test the safelight(s) as follows: Make a test strip (pages 55–57) with no negative in the enlarger and the lens stopped down three or four times. You will get a strip of flat tones, and you want the exposure time for a light-to-medium gray. Now turn out the safelight(s) and give another strip of paper single exposure: for this desired tone. Still in the dark, line up six nickels or quarters on the strip.

Turn on the safelight(s) and after one minute remove a coin. Every minute thereafter remove

another coin, until they are all gone. Then turn off the safelight(s) and process the strip in the dark, using a two-minute developing time. After fixing, see how many coin silhouettes there are on the strip. If there are none it means your safelight is safe for at least six minutes with the type of paper used for making the test. If you see three the light is safe for only three minutes or a little more, etc.

Ordinarily, three or four minutes is all the safe time you need for exposing and developing a print, especially if you learn to work fast.

If you have a serious light-leak problem, test the safelight(s) first—at night, when you know there is no light leaking in. Then, in the daytime, run another safelight test to see if the leaking light and the safelight *together* are causing fog. If you get fog in less than three or four minutes, run another test for the light leak alone, with the safelight(s) turned off during the whole procedure. If you still get fog too soon it means that your darkroom isn't very safe to work in during the daytime, but there are things you can do to improve matters.

If you are getting fog from a light leak, from a safelight, or from the two working together, here are some things you can do:

Plug the light leak better
Work only at night
Use a slower enlarging paper
Get a lower-wattage bulb for your safelight
Take less time to get your paper exposed and into the developer
Develop your prints face down in the tray
Develop them in the dark, turning on the safelight only for periodic inspections
Use an anti-fogging agent in the developer

Benzotriazole is the commonly used anti-fogging agent. It is sold as Kodak Anti-Fog no. 1 in both pill and powder form. The powder is by far the more economical, though the initial cost (for four ounces) is a bit higher. It is used for paper that has been fogged over all by age, heat, and humidity—also to help solve the light-leak and safelight problem. It works very well indeed, but one shouldn't overwork the idea.

With fog tests to check their efficacy, you can use some or all of these tricks and work successfully in an area with quite a bit of light spilling in, though it might be easier to light-trap it properly (pages 11–12).

Use the same techniques to see if there is too much light leaking in to permit you to develop film, but stop the lens all the way down for the multiple-tone test strip, making your exposures on a strip of film instead of on paper. You can pull out lengths of it without opening the cassette, and use the rest for shooting pictures. If you use roll film or cartridge load, buy a 35-mm cassette of discount, out-of-date film for your tests. Ask your dealer for some with the same speed as the film you generally use.

With film, the safelight(s) should be turned off during the whole procedure, because we already know that it would cause fog and are only interested in what the leaking light will do. Use Dektol 1:2 again (at 68 to 75 F for film) and develop for a minute and a half. Again, the number of visible coin silhouettes will tell you how much safe time you have, if any. If you have as much as three or four minutes, you should be all right, provided that you pop your film right into the developing tank as soon as it has been loaded onto the reel.

However, you can get by with even more light leakage if you take precautionary steps. Of course you can use a changing bag (page 13) but that costs money. If you work in a room as dark as you can get it, with just a moderate amount of leakage, there are two effective substitutes for such a bag; and they will cost you nothing. One, load your film reels and put them in the tank under a dark coat or blanket. Two, get a stout cardboard grocery box with a top that is in good shape and cut two tight armholes in adjacent sides, one per side. Put your film cassettes, bottle opener, reels, and developing tank in it, then tape down the top. Shove your arms through the holes, load the reels, put them in the tank, and

put the top on. Then you can safely open the box. With these two systems you can counteract a rather serious light-leak problem, but it wouldn't be smart to push your luck too far.

• Developing Film by Inspection

There will be times when you know or strongly suspect that you have made rather large errors in exposing your film. Two common reasons for this are forgetting to set the correct film-speed number on your exposure meter and having to guess the correct exposure in light so dim that the meter in your camera won't register it. In the first case, you can easily figure out whether all of your film is over- or underexposed, but your guesswork exposures may go either way. In either case, you don't know what developing time you should use, because the normal time should be paired only with normal exposures. It will make overexposures too dense (dark, or heavy) and underexposures too thin (clear, or light), so you have to abandon the normal time. But then what do you do?

You simply develop the film by inspection, that is by looking at it periodically for short intervals under a Kodak no. 3 (dark-green) safelight with a 15-watt bulb in it. Even though film is sensitive to green light (panchromatic film, that is) you can do this safely because it loses much of its light sensitivity during development and the green light is very dim. The rule is that you shouldn't start inspecting until half of the normal development time has elapsed. However, if you think that the film is heavily overexposed you may have to start a bit sooner, for you may wish to put it in the fixer before the halfway point.

For a considerably brighter green light, also quite safe, you might buy a "Fotopanhandler," made by Erco. As the name telegraphically implies, one uses it for handling (inspecting) panchromatic photosensitive materials. Since it has solid-state circuitry, there are no bulbs to replace and it will probably work for years without giving difficulty. Furthermore, it initially costs very little more than the Kodak safelight setup and just a few pennies a year to operate.

If you intend to develop some film by inspection you should set up an auxiliary *tray* of developer, filled to the very top, diluted 1:1, and at the right temperature. Also have a tray of hypo (fixer) handy. If necessary, you can then pull the whole roll of film off the developing reel at the halfway time. With scissors, you can start cutting off the frames (or strips of frames) that have developed long enough and immediately putting them in the hypo. You can continue developing the remainder of the film spaghetti fashion in the developer tray, just stirring it around gently to insure even development. If you guard against fingernails, this technique will give you excellent results, so don't worry about the incongruity of it.

As another preliminary to inspecting film, you should turn off all lights except the inspection light several minutes before the midway point, in order to get your eyes dark-accommodated. Even with the Erco light the illumination level is low, so doing this is a must. By prior experimentation you can learn precisely how long it takes your eyes to fully adapt.

Now we come to the hard part: how can you tell in such dim light when a frame or roll has developed long enough? The sad, tough answer is that you can learn only through experience. You have to find out by *doing*. However, there are some general guidelines. If a roll has developed long enough, all the frames will usually (but not always) show up clearly under the green light as dark rectangles when viewed from the emulsion side. When you look at the other side they may show up a little bit, and there may be some little dark details showing here and there. These record the highlights in your pictures and will print as whites or near whites.

The best way to learn what the negatives should look like under green light is to get some practice on film you know to be normally exposed. Use both the time-and-temperature method and development by inspection for the same roll, but rely on the time to tell you when to discard the developer and pour in the hypo. Thus when you inspect the film at the halfway point you will know you are looking at frames that haven't developed far enough. When you examine it at the end of the time, just before fixation, you will know you are inspecting frames that are just right. Inspecting film after fixation isn't the same thing at all, but you might try it just to see what the difference is.

Lots of people, including many professionals and custom-lab technicians, do development by inspection, and this is the way they all learned how. There is just no other way to learn except by doing.

You now need to know approximately how far you can go with "jerking" film or "pushing" it —with cutting the developing time or extending it. It is quite safe to either cut the time in half or double it, though you can actually go further in both directions. However, there can be a serious quality fall-off with extended pushing, but this depends to a large degree on the visual graphics of your subject matter. By doubling the time or more, you may end up with contrasty and grainy negatives that are difficult or impossible to print well, even if the exposure and developing times are correctly paired.

With a half-normal developing time or less, correctly paired with overexposure, there is no such problem, though your negatives may be quite flat and require a contrasty printing paper (contrast increases with developing time, temperature, and agitation—and vice versa).

If you would like to know rather accurately the ranges of over- and underexposure that can be compensated for by shorter or longer developing times, you should run tests such as the one described on pages 63 through 66 in my book *Beginner's Guide to Photography*. To describe the test in detail here would go beyond the intended scope of this Appendix. However, we can make some rough pairings of exposure and developing time:

For $4\times$ to $16\times$ *over*exposure (two to four stops), develop one half the normal time. For the

$16\times$ you might even go as low as one third the time.

For $4\times$ to $16\times$ *under*exposure (two to four stops), develop twice the normal time. For the $16\times$ under you might even go as high as two and one half times.

These data will serve well as a rough guide, which is about all that you can use anyway, because when you *have* to use inspection development you are dealing mainly with exposures of unknown quantity. In order to learn to recognize these unknown quantities, it would be wise to do quite a bit of practice developing on correctly exposed rolls and deliberately under- and overexposing on a roll or two just for practice in seeing what comes out.

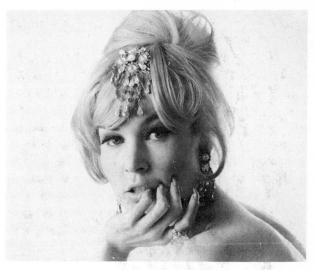

• How to Diffuse (Soften) Prints

Some prints look a little better if the fine details aren't too sharp. This is particularly true of delicate portraits of children and young women. If they are just a little bit soft, the blemishes (pimples, blackheads, and acne scars) tend to disappear or lose their power to attract our attention. Graininess is either lessened or eliminated altogether. Skin takes on a kind of creamy smoothness that is quite attractive. Fortunately, getting this diffuse softness is no problem at all.

The only tool you need is a small piece of cellophane, such as plastic food wrap or the wrapping from a package of cigarettes. You wad it into a tight ball, then flatten it out again, which leaves it very wrinkled. During the print expo-

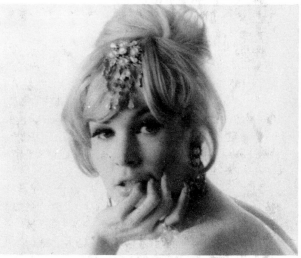

Print A is a low-contrast print that has had no diffusion whatever. Print B was diffused with cellophane for half of the printing exposure time, print C for the entire time.

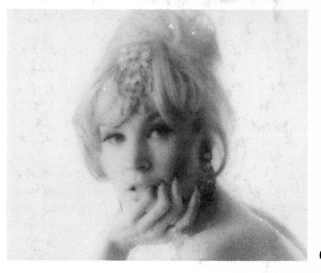

sure, you wave it around under the lens, at a distance of about two inches, for all or part of the exposure time.

Part-time diffusion gives us a moderate softening and blurring effect, which is usually (but not always) best, while full-time gives us considerably more. For even greater diffusion, use two or three layers of wrinkled plastic for the whole time. The technique is just as simple as it sounds, so don't complicate it in your mind.

Diffusion not only softens a print but flattens it, too. A flat, soft print that is not very dark may look good, while one that is too dark may look muddy. However, if you want softness without a loss of contrast you can use a printing paper one or two contrast grades higher than you would usually use for your negative. You could even print a no. 2 negative on a Brovira no. 6 and bring down the contrast to the desired level by cellophane diffusion.

You can also do local diffusion if you like, softening selected parts of an image and letting the remainder print straight. Again, the technique is very easy. Make yourself a special diffusion dodger, using a wrinkled cellophane shape instead of a cardboard disk. Also, make yourself a wrinkled cellophane "burning-in card," using a piece of plastic quite a bit larger. You can make it easier to handle by taping it to a frame made of light cardboard. Cut a hole in the middle so that you can do straight printing through it while the rest of the image is being diffused and flattened. With the dodger, you can diffuse small areas, for all or part of the exposure time, while the rest of the picture prints straight.

Though cellophane diffusion is used mainly for portraits, it also goes well with gothic or romantic landscapes. It also adapts itself to communicating the ideas of spring and youth, and well fits ethereal and dreamy concepts. Happily, it is about as easy a technique as you can find in photography.

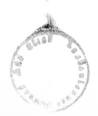